THE RATIFICATION OF THE CONSTITUTION
AND
THE BILL OF RIGHTS

THE

RATIFICATION

OF THE CONSTITUTION

AND

THE BILL OF RIGHTS

Peter Schrag
Amherst College

NEW DIMENSIONS IN AMERICAN HISTORY
Developed by the
SECONDARY SCHOOL HISTORY COMMITTEE

Van R. Halsey
Amherst College
GENERAL EDITOR

D. C. HEATH AND COMPANY BOSTON

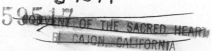

New Dimensions in American History

Introduction

The study of history is one of many ways that man organizes his experience. He undertakes it in order better to understand himself and his relations to others around him. Properly conceived, it is not a quest for "facts" and "trends" upon which there is universal agreement but a search for human understanding. Approaching its study, man cannot expect to find all the answers. Much that he would like to know he finds inaccessible; many of the "facts" he thinks he knows turn out to be rooted in uncertainty; the assumption he starts with, and his own biases and interests, affect his conclusions. But in approaching it he uses the tools, within a definable area, by which man seeks everywhere to cut into reality. He must decide what material is relevant to his particular investigation. He must analyze and organize that material. He must frame hypotheses, form generalizations, and learn to perceive their limits. Above all, at every stage, he must ask the right questions.

Believing that the study of history can profitably be approached in this way at the secondary school level, the Secondary School History Committee, a group of secondary school and college history teachers, has produced a series of teaching units, of which the following is one. The units vary as to type: some are topical in nature; some are essentially problems, focusing in depth on a particular episode; some deal with a particular period of historic time. But all in common are built primarily out of source material —the raw material with which the historian has to deal. And all attempt to present those materials in such a way that the student will be invited to see historical development and local events not as isolated phenomena, but within the context of the larger world and the universal human situation.

It is the hope of the Committee that the units will make it possible for the teacher to present history not simply as a collection of facts to be mastered, but as a rich and rewarding intellectual experience. Rather than asking the student to remember isolated facts, the units encourage him to seek the possible meaning, pattern, and coherence among a group of facts. What is lost in traditional "coverage" will be, it is hoped, more than compensated for by making what is covered meaningful; while at the same time the student will develop habits of mind which in the long run must prove far more useful to him in the pursuit of knowledge than any random collection of covered "facts." As for the traditional notion that chronology can only be taught by "coverage," it is the Committee's feeling that it might better be approached by giving the student a more clear-cut and functional notion of relationships such as those of cause and effect. Then, in the course of asking the right questions, he must inevitably seek out chronology not as something to be learned, but because he has a use for it in answering his own questions.

The units vary in length and method. They have been designed to be used either in conjunction with other material, or as a course by themselves. Most require two weeks of work, although some have been planned for less. Each is accompanied by a teacher's edition which suggests one method—though by no means the only one—of teaching it. As for method, each unit in one way or another asks the student, through a series of relatively simple questions, to construct and to develop his powers of critical thinking and analysis. Each asks him to formulate hypotheses, frequently in writing, and to refine the hypotheses in the light of subsequent evidence. Each begins with limited questions about specific pieces of evidence and encourages the student to move outward toward some usable generalizations which will have relevance and meaning for his own approach to the problems and complexities of the world in which he lives.

CONTENTS

PREFACE

The Ratification of the Constitution and the Bill of Rights

The Constitution of the United States was drafted at a convention in Philadelphia during the spring and summer of 1787. This convention drew many of the leading men of the age. Its president was George Washington. Delegates included Alexander Hamilton, James Madison, James Wilson, Benjamin Franklin, Roger Sherman, Robert Morris and Gouverneur Morris. Every state but one, Rhode Island, was represented. However, several men whose names you will recognize from prior studies of American history were absent. Among them were John Adams and Thomas Jefferson who were serving in diplomatic positions in Europe and Patrick Henry who declined to serve.

The convention completed its work on September 17. On that date most, though not all, of the delegates signed their names to the draft Constitution. Through Washington they asked the Congress of the Confederation to request the states to call special ratifying conventions. The Constitution itself provided that when nine states had ratified it, it would go into effect for those states.

Within a year all the states except Rhode Island had called conventions. In some of these conventions the Constitution was approved with hardly a dissent. In one state, North Carolina, the vote of the convention was tantamount to rejection, and in several it became the

1

subject of a bitter struggle. Among these were New York, Massachusetts, and Virginia.

The struggle for ratification generated some of the most important political writing in American history, and it proved an occasion when many of the fundamental political and social ideas in the American tradition were aired.

The sections which you will be asked to read are drawn largely from these writings or from the speeches made about the Constitution at the time. By and large the readings will not tell you what "happened" in the same way that a textbook would. Instead, you will be asked to do very much the same thing that the historian does. You will read documents, and you will be asked to formulate your own history of the period.

If you have never worked with this kind of material before you may find the work difficult and sometimes frustrating. You may find yourself asking: "Tell me what really happened: What are the facts?" You should remember, if you are having such difficulties, that even today historians do not agree on all of the crucial aspects of this, or any other, period. Imagine yourself to be a kind of detective faced with a collection of clues, some of which will help you decide on the "real" story, but remember also that, in part, the real story depends on the person reconstructing it.

In planning this unit, it was generally assumed that high school students are capable of mature work, that they need not be led by the hand. Consistent with this idea, this manual provides you with a short bibliography. Look it over before you proceed far into the unit. You are not responsible for reading these works, but it is hoped that you will use the bibliography to amplify points which you feel are not sufficiently clarified in the assigned readings. In addition, you will find a brief chronology of events at the back of the manual. You need not memorize it, but you must have it in mind as you do your work. If you feel you need to refer to a general history book or a text, your teacher may be able to provide one.

I

INTRODUCTION

Unlike most of the sections which follow, the passage below was not written by a contemporary of the Constitutional Convention. It was written in 1924 by a high school student in California who was a finalist in the National Oratorical Contest. The contest was sponsored by a number of American newspapers. Participants had to choose the Constitution as a subject. Each year's winner was awarded a substantial cash prize.

This section is included not to test your patriotism or that of the writer. It is here, rather, to give you a chance to ask such questions as: What is history? Where does one find it? How is it made? What is the difference between history and patriotism?

These men did not walk alone on that spring morning into that Philadelphia Convention. There walked in with them the thousands upon thousands of shadowy nameless persons who had through the centuries worked toward liberty and order. There were those struggling figures who through years of labor and agony and sacrifice had been working out the priceless practical principles of Anglo-Saxon liberty.

And so the fathers of our Constitution embodied in that instrument the spirit of the Magna Charta and the petition of rights and the bill of rights and the habeas corpus act, of all that made the people of England great, and an adaptation of those great principles of American life through the practical working of 150 years of American government.

Then, at the end of four months, these men, after discussing, debating, and deliberating, brought forth the most finished, polished and balanced relation between a people and their government that the human mind has ever conceived. . .

From *Oratory*, Randolph Leigh, Ed., 1927, Putnam & Sons, N. Y.

II

THE
"CRITICAL"
PERIOD

The documents in this section all relate to the years 1783–87. Some are from newspapers, some are letters written during the period and some are official documents or records of government action.

These materials are provided to set the scene for the events which follow. Naturally all that you have studied about American history, about government, politics, economics should help give you a framework in your readings. The source readings in this section, however, pertain directly to the time immediately preceding the Philadelphia Convention. In reading, you might ask yourself whether the opinions voiced here were identical or whether there was disagreement. You might try to establish not so much the details but the general ideas with which this material deals.

In reading this, keep in mind the fact that American leaders of the 1780's were not men living on a desert island, cut off from the vital forces and ideas that swept the world. Remember that a few years before, Americans had fought and won a revolutionary struggle against Great Britain; that they had fought this war not so much in the name of what they considered uniquely American ideas but in the name of the rights of Englishmen and of rights that they considered universal. In one form or another, Americans had expressed their ideals of government for many years. State constitutions, letters, political tracts, and petitions were colored by these notions. They appeared in the Declaration of Independence, in Thomas Paine's *Common Sense,* even in the writings of the Puritans of the seventeenth century.

During the period after the Revolution the government of the United States was operating under the Articles of Confederation. These articles, "America's first constitution," included the following:

A. Articles of Confederation and Perpetual Union between the States of New Hampshire, Massachusetts, etc.

ARTICLE I. The style of this Confedcracy shall be "The United States of America."

ARTICLE II. Each state retains its sovereignty, freedom and independence, and every power, jurisdiction and right, which is not by this Confederation expressly delegated to the United States in Congress assembled.

ARTICLE III. The said States hereby severally enter into a firm league of friendship with each other, for their common defense, the security of their liberties . . . .

ARTICLE V. For the more convenient management of the general interests of the United States, delegates shall be annually appointed in such manner as the legislature of each State shall direct, to meet in Congress . . . with a power reserved to each state to recall its delegates, or any of them, at any time within the year, and to send others in their stead. . . .

ARTICLE VIII. All charges of war and all other expenses that shall be incurred for the common defense or general welfare . . . shall be defrayed out of a common treasury, which shall be supplied by the several states in proportion to the value of all land within each State. . . . The taxes . . . shall be laid and levied by the authority and direction of the legislature of the several states. . . .

The Articles were written in 1777–78, ratified in 1781 and remained in effect until 1789.

B. *Boston, October 27, 1783.*

Last Wednesday arrived the ship Robin Hood, Capt. Smith, from London. From the London papers to the 11th of September we have extracted the following FRESH INTELLIGENCE. London, September 9. *Copy of a letter received by the Right Hon. The Lord Mayor.*

My Lord

. . . The Definitive Treaty (of Peace) with the United States of America was signed at Paris the third instant by David Hartley, Esq., his Majesty's Plenipotentiary and the Plenipotentiaries of those States. . . .

> I am with great respect, etc.
> C. J. Fox
> *(Prime Minister of Great Britain)*

From *Boston Independent Ledger* and *American Advertiser* (1783).

C. *London, August 2, 1783*

It seems that the Americans who revolted rather than pay taxes to the mother country are now averse to paying any taxes and having overturned the government under which they were born and bred are unwilling to submit to any kind of government . . . .

Quoted from London papers in *The Boston Independent Chronicle* of October 23, 1783.

D. Congress stand in a very delicate and embarrassing situation. On the one hand they are blamed for not doing what they have no means of doing; on the other their attempts are branded with the imputations of a spirit of encroachment and a lust of power.

In these circumstances, it is the duty of all those who have the welfare of the community at heart to unite their efforts to direct the attention of the people to the true source of the public disorders—the want of efficient general government,—and to impress upon them this conviction, that these States, to be happy must have a stronger bond of Union and a Confederation capable of drawing forth the resources of the country. This will be more laudable an occupation than that of cavilling against measures the imperfection of which is the necessary results of the (Articles of Confederation).

Alexander Hamilton, 1783.

E. It now rests with the states by the line of conduct they mean to adopt, to make this Country great, happy and respectable; or to sink it into littleness; worse perhaps, into Anarchy and confusion; for certain I am, that unless adequate Powers are given to Congress for the *general* purposes of the Federal Union that we shall soon moulder into dust and become contemptable in the

Eyes of Europe, if we are not made the sport of their Politicks; to suppose that the general concern of this Country can be directed by thirteen heads, or one head without competent powers, is a solecism, the bad effects of which every Man who has had the practical knowledge to judge from, that I have, is fully convinced of; tho' none perhaps has felt them in so forcible, and distressing a degree. The People at large, and at a distance from the theatre of Action, who only know that the Machine was kept in motion, and that they are at last arrived at the first object of their Wishes are satisfied with the event, without investigating the causes of the slow progress to it, or of the Expences which have accrued and which they now seem unwilling to pay; great part of which has arisen from that want of energy in the Federal Constitution which I am complaining of, and which I wish to see given to it by a Convention of the People, instead of hearing it remarked that as we have worked through an arduous Contest with the Powers Congress already have (but which, by the by, have been gradually diminishing) why should they be invested with more?

George Washington in a letter, July 8, 1783.

F. By all the accounts I read and hear, which merit attention, the people (of America) are very happy, and getting fast into flourishing circumstances in their agriculture, commerce, and fisheries. May God prosper them all!

John Adams (from Paris), 1784.

G. The policy of our country is not perfect. The most fatal and egregious fault of all is leaving (the) debt in Holland and France unfunded. . . . This single step may protect us from a war and confute forever the numberless calumnies which circulate now . . . I have hitherto paid the interest in Holland out of the principal; this will by and by be impracticable, and then such a clamor and obloquy will succeed as to make us all ashamed of ourselves. How will it be possible to vindicate the faith and honor of our country?

John Adams (American Ambassador in London), 1785.

H. *Resolved,* That a deputation . . . be appointed to repair to and confer with the Legislatures of Rhode Island . . . New York and Georgia . . . to state to them the public embarrassments for want of money, and urge on them the necessity of an immediate compliance with the recommendations (requesting funds) of April 18, 1783.

March 15, 1785, in the Continental Congress.

I. . . . It is with regret we are constrained to observe that the collection of General Taxes in the several States goes on with so much languor, and meets with such obstructions, that in our opinion a Sufficient Sum in Specie will not be paid into the Public Treasury during the present year . . . to defray the Ordinary Expenses of Government.

State of the quotas, with the amounts paid and Balances due of 8 million dollars required by Act of Congress of 30th October, 1781 . . .

STATES	QUOTAS	AMOUNTS PAID	BALANCES DUE
N. H.	373,598	7,679	365,918
Mass.	1,307,596	363,036	944,559
. . . .	. .	. .	. .
Dollars	8,000,000	2,220,911	5,779,088

(*fractions of dollars are omitted*)

Report from the Board of Treasury to the Continental Congress, June 1785.

J. Your newspapers (in England) are filled with accounts of distress and miseries, that these States are plunged into since their separation from Great Britain. You may believe me when I tell you that there is no truth in these accounts. I find all property in lands and houses augmented vastly in value; that of houses in towns at least fourfold. The crops have been plentiful, and yet the produce sells high, to the great profit of the farmer. At the same time, all imported goods sell at low rates, some cheaper than the first cost. Working people have plenty of employ and high pay for their labor.

Benjamin Franklin, just returned from Europe, to a correspondent in England, October 27, 1785.

K. The selfishness and corruption of Europe I have no doubt about, and therefore wish most sincerely that our free Republics may not suffer themselves to be changed and wrongly wrought upon by the corrupt maxims of policy that pervade European Councils—where artful and refined plausibility is forever called in to aid the most pernicious designs. It would seem as if there were a general jealousy beyond the water, of the powerful effects to be derived from Republican virtue here, and so we hear a constant cry from thence, echoed & re-echoed here by all Expectants from the Treasury of the United States—That Congress must have more power—That we cannot be secure & happy until Congress command implicitly both purse & sword. So that our confederation must be perpetually changing to answer sinister views in the greater part, until every fence is thrown down that was designed to protect & cover the rights of Mankind. It is a melancholy consideration that many wise & good men have, somehow or other, fallen in with these ruinous opinions. I think Sir that the first maxim of a man who loves liberty should be, never to grant to Rulers an atom of power that is not most clearly & indispensably necessary for the safety and well being of Society. To say that these Rulers are revocable, and holding their places during pleasure may not be supposed to design evil for self-aggrandizement, is affirming what I cannot easily admit. Look to history and see how often the liberties of mankind have been oppressed & ruined by the same delusive hopes & falacious reasoning. The fact is, that power poisons the mind of its possessor and aids him to remove the shackles that restrain itself. To be sure, all things human must partake of human infirmity, and therefore the Confederation should not be presumptuously called an infallible system for all times and all situations—but tho' this is true, yet as it is a great and fundamental system of Union & Security, no change should be admitted until proved to be necessary by the fairest fullest & most mature experience. Upon these principles I have ever been opposed to the 5 P Cent imposts, My idea is still that of the Confederation, Fix the sum, Apportion it & let every State by its own means, and in its own way faithfully & honestly make its payment. That the now federal mode of apportionment is productive of delay, of great expence, and still liable to frequent change, is certain. And therefore I see no inconvenience in so far altering the Confederation as to make the Rule of Apportionment lie upon the numbers as stated in the recommendation of Congress upon that Subject. But I can never agree that this Body shall dictate the mode of Taxation, or that the collection shall in any manner be subject to Congressional controul. It is said that this will more effectually secure the Revenue—But how so? if a spirit prevails to neglect a duty imposed by the Confederation, may not the same spirit render abortive at any time Acts passed for granting the Impost? Besides that we are depending for the payment of our debts upon uncertainty, when the most certain revenues of the State ought to be appropriated for that purpose. Whilst every good man wishes great punctuality to prevail in the payment of debts, he must at the same time condemn and discourage large importations which impoverish by increasing the balance of trade against us. So that from this system we are to expect our greatest good from our greatest evil. A good physician will tell you that contrary indications of cure threaten danger to human life, and by a just parity of reason, contrary indications threaten danger to the Political body. But happily for us, our political disease admits of simple remedies for its cure, if rightly judged of, and wisely practised upon. Let it be therefore the effort of every Patriot to encourage a punctual payment of each State's quota of the fœderal demand, and let the money be found in ways most agreeable to the circumstances of every State. This is the plan of the Confederation, and this I own will be mine, until more satisfactory experience has proved its inefficacy.

Richard Henry Lee (president of Congress) to Samuel Morse, 1785.

L. Our national debt is small, our resources almost untouched, and our means of discharging it, if wisely improved, nearly inexhaustible; . . .

Letter to the Salem, Mass., *Gazette,* signed "Honestus," 1785.

M. There is not upon the face of the earth a body of people more happy or rising into consequence with more rapid strides than the inhabitants of the United States of America. Population is increasing, new houses building, new lands clearing, new settlements forming, and new manufactures establishing with a rapidity beyond conception, and what is more, the people are well clad, well fed and well housed.

Charles Thomson, secretary of Congress, to Jefferson (U. S. Minister in Paris), 1786.

N. The policy of [Great Britain] (to say nothing of other nations) has shut against us the channels without which our trade with her must be a losing one;* and she has consequently the triumph, as we have the chagrin, of seeing accomplished her prophetic threats, that our independence should forfeit commercial advantages for which it would not recompence us with any new channels of trade. What is to be done? Must we remain passive victims to foreign politics, or shall we exert the lawful means which our independence has put into our hands of extorting redress? The very question would be an affront to every Citizen who loves his Country. What, then, are these means? Retaliating regulations of trade only. How are these to be ef-

* This is a reference to restrictions on American ships and seamen in British ports. Ed.

fectuated? only by harmony in the measures of the States. How is this harmony to be obtained? only by an acquiescence of all the States in the opinion of a reasonable majority. If Congress as they are now constituted, can not be trusted with the power of digesting and enforcing this opinion, let them be otherwise constituted: let their numbers be encreased, let them be chosen oftener, and let their period of service be shortened; or if any better medium than Congress can be proposed by which the wills of the States may be concentrated, let it be substituted; or lastly let no regulation of trade adopted by Congress be in force until it shall have been ratified by a certain proportion of the States. But let us not sacrifice the end to the means: let us not rush on certain ruin in order to avoid a possible danger. I conceive it to be of great importance that the defects of the fœderal system should be amended, not only because such amendments will make it better answer the purpose for which it was instituted, but because I apprehend danger to its very existence from a continuance of defects which expose a part if not the whole of the empire to severe distress. The suffering part, even when the minor part, can not long respect a Government which is too feeble to protect their interests: But when the suffering part comes to be the major part, and they despair of seeing a protecting energy given to the General Government, from what motives is their allegiance to be any longer expected. Should G. B. persist in the machinations which distress us; and seven or eight of the States be hindered by the others from obtaining relief by fœderal means, I own, I tremble at the anti-fœderal expedients into which the former may be tempted.

Madison to Monroe, 1785.

O. Is it possible with such an example before our eyes of impotency in the federal system, to remain sceptical with regard to the necessity of infusing more energy into it?* A Government cannot long stand which is obliged in the ordinary course of its administration to court a compliance with its *constitutional* acts, from a member not of the most powerful order, situated within the immediate verge of authority, and apprised of every circumstance which should remonstrate against disobedience. The question whether it be possible and worth while to preserve the Union of the States must be speedily decided some way or other. Those who are indifferent to its preservation would do well to look forward to the consequences of its extinction. The prospect to my eye is a gloomy one indeed. I am glad to hear that the opposition to the impost is likely to be overcome. It is an encouragement to persevere in good measures. I am afraid at the same time that the other auxiliary resources it will be overrated by the States, and slacken the regular efforts of taxation. It is also materially short of the power which Congress ought to have with regard to Trade. It leaves the door unshut agst a commercial warfare among the States, our trade exposed to foreign machinations, and the distresses of an unfavorable balance very little checked.

Madison to Monroe, 1786.

Frequently people in one state were forced to pay duties to another state on goods imported through that state. James Madison had been actively engaged in attempts to strengthen the Congress of the Confederation. He hoped the states would grant an impost (a duty on

* This is a reference to New Jersey's refusal to pay a requisition levied by Congress. Ed.

goods brought into the country) and that they would cede the power to regulate interstate and foreign commerce to Congress.

P. The American States as to their general internal policies are *not* united; there is no supreme power at their head; they are in a perfect state of nature and independence as to each other; each is at liberty to fight its neighbor, and there is no sovereign to call forth the powers of the continent to quell the dispute or punish the aggressor . . . the whole is restricted by cobwebs and shadows, the jest and ridicule of the world.

Noah Webster, *Sketches of American Policy*, Hartford, 1785, p. 37.

In 1786 a group of Federalist poets known as the Hartford Wits published a long work of verse which contained:

Q. But know, ye favor'd race, one potent head
   Must rule your states, and strike your foes with dread,
   The finance regulate, the trade control
   Live through the empire, and accord the whole.

The Anarchiad, Hartford, 1786, p. 63.

In 1786 and early 1787, debtors in Massachusetts and elsewhere pressed for the issuance of paper money. Some states, notably Rhode Island, had been issuing some form of paper money. The legislature of Massachusetts, controlled by coastal merchants, many of whom were creditors of the farmer debtors, resisted the pressure. Farmers were heavily taxed and some faced debtor's prison.

In Massachusetts they took matters in their own hands and prevented courts from sitting; a group, under Daniel Shays of Pelham, made an attempt to seize the Federal arsenal at Springfield. The attempt failed.

R. We have been in alarm for twelve days past. Last week the insurgents in this county and the county of Berkshire were collecting those from Middlesex and Bristol, to stop the courts of Common Pleas and Sessions at Cambridge. Their place of rendezvous was Shrewsbury. By the best accounts they were collecting Monday, Tuesday, Wednesday and Thursday . . . They were headed by Shaise who it is said, has about 100 from Hampshire . . . .

From *Boston Independent Chronicle and Universal Advertiser,* December 7, 1786.

S. . . . The expedition of Genl. Lincoln against the insurgents has effectually dispersed the main body of them. It appears, however, that there are still some detachments which remain to be subdued & that the Government of Massachusetts considers very strong precautions as necessary against further eruptions. The principal incendiaries have unluckily made off. No money is paid into the public treasury; no respect is paid to the federal authority. Not a single state complies with the requisitions; several pass them over in silence, and some positively reject them. The payments ever since the peace have been decreasing, and of late fall short even of the pittance necessary for the Civil list of the Confederacy. It is not possible that a government can last long under the circumstances. If the approaching convention should not agree on some remedy, I am persuaded that some very different arrangement will ensue. The late turbulent scenes in

Massachusetts and infamous ones in Rhode Island have done expressible injury in that part of the United States.

Letter from Madison to Edmund Pendleton, Governor of Virginia, February 24, 1787.

T. ... the situation of the general government, if it can be called a government, is shaken to its foundation, and liable to be overturned by every blast. In a word it is at an end; and, unless a remedy is soon applied, anarchy and confusion will inevitably ensue.

Washington to Jefferson, May 30, 1787. (By this time the convention had begun and Washington had been elected its presiding officer.)

U. The expectations and hopes of all the Union centre in this convention. God grant that we may be able to concert effectual means of preserving our country from the evils which threaten us.

George Mason of Virginia to his son from Philadelphia, May 20, 1787.

V. Vices of the Political System of the United States
   1. Failure of the States to comply with the Constitutional Requisitions.
   2. Encroachments by the States on the federal authority.
   3. Violations of the law of nations and of treaties.
   4. Trespasses of the states on the rights of each other.
   5. Want of concert in matters where common interest requires it.
   6. Want of Guaranty to the States of their Constitutions and laws against internal violence.

7. Want of sanction to the laws, and of coercion in the Government of the Confederacy.
8. Want of ratification by the people of the articles of Confederation.
9. Multiplicity of the laws in the several States.
10. Mutability of the laws of the States.

Notes made by Madison, April 1787.

III

THE

CONSTITUTION

A convention met at Annapolis, Maryland in December 1786 to discuss granting powers over interstate and foreign commerce to the Congress of the Confederation. However, only a few states were represented. Lacking the representation to act definitively, the delegates petitioned their states to ask Congress to call a convention the following year to consider general revisions in the Articles of Confederation. It was this request which led to the convention in Philadelphia that drew the Constitution.

The convention itself was closed (only rumors filtered out of Philadelphia during the summer) but Madison and others kept notes of the proceedings which were later edited and published by the historian Max Farrand as *The Records of the Federal Convention* (1911). The convention was presented with two major schemes, one proposed by delegates from Virginia (The Virginia Plan), the other by delegates from some of the smaller states (The New Jersey Plan). The former became the basis of the Constitution, but only after several compromises had been made. The attitudes of the delegates themselves varied (many changed their minds on specific points during the summer) yet they shared many of the views held by all sophisticated men of their time. You will get some idea of those attitudes by reading *The Federalist,* the works of John Adams (selections from both appear in ensuing sections of this pamphlet), and the literature of the American Revolution.

The reading in this section is the Constitution of the United States (no need now to read the amendments). You need not memorize the details, but try to understand its general outline, especially in light of the reading so far. As you read, you should know that the Constitution itself represented several major compromises:

1. A compromise between large and small states. The former wished representation in the government to be based on population, the latter on states. As a result, states were represented equally in the Senate. The lower house was chosen on the basis of population.

2. A compromise between North and South in representation and taxation. The North wished taxation to be proportioned according to population but the South resisted counting slaves in determining taxes. The North, on the other hand, wanted Negroes to be given less weight in determining representation in the House. The resulting compromise specified that for both representation and taxation five Negroes would be counted the equivalent of three whites—the "three-fifths compromise."

In reading, bear in mind the general provisions of the Articles of Confederation and the complaints directed against the Articles.

The
Constitution
of the
United States

The Federal Constitution

AS AGREED UPON BY THE CONVENTION
SEPTEMBER 17, 1787

WE, THE PEOPLE OF THE UNITED STATES, in order to form a more perfect union, establish justice, insure domestic tranquillity, provide for the common defence, promote the general welfare, and secure the blessings of liberty to ourselves and our posterity, do ordain and establish this Constitution for the United States of America.

ARTICLE I. SECTION 1. All legislative powers herein granted shall be vested in a Congress of the United States which shall consist of a Senate and House of Representatives.

SECTION 2. The House of Representatives shall be composed of members chosen every second year by the people of the several States, and the electors in each State shall have the qualifications requisite for electors of the most numerous branch of the State legislature.

No person shall be a representative who shall not have attained to the age of twenty-five years, and been seven years a citizen of the United States, and who shall not, when elected, be an inhabitant of that State in which he shall be chosen.

Representatives and direct taxes shall be apportioned among the several States which may be included within this Union, according to their respective numbers, which shall be determined by adding to the whole number of free persons, including those bound to service for a term of years, and excluding Indians not taxed, three fifths of all other persons. The actual enumeration shall be made within three years after the first meeting of the Congress of the United States, and within every subsequent term of ten years, in such manner as they shall by law direct. The number of representatives shall not exceed one for every thirty thousand but each State shall have at least one representative; and until such enumeration shall be made, the State of New Hampshire shall be entitled to choose three; Massachusetts, eight; Rhode Island and Providence Plantations, one; Connecticut, five; New York, six; New Jersey, four; Pennsylvania, eight; Delaware, one; Maryland, six; Virginia, ten; North Carolina, five; South Carolina, five; and Georgia, three.

When vacancies happen in the representation from any State, the executive authority thereof shall issue writs of election to fill such vacancies.

The House of Representatives shall choose their Speaker and other officers, and shall have the sole power of impeachment.

SECTION 3. The Senate of the United States shall be composed of two Senators from each State, chosen by the legislature thereof, for six years; and each Senator shall have one vote.

Immediately after they shall be assembled in consequence of the first election, they shall be divided as equally as may be into three classes. The seats of the Senators of the first class shall be vacated at the expiration of the second year, of the second class at the expiration of the fourth year, and of the third class at the expiration of the sixth year, so that one-third may be chosen every second year; and if vacancies happen by resignation or otherwise during the recess of the legislature of any State, the executive thereof may make temporary appointments until the next meeting of the legislature, which shall then fill such vacancies.

No person shall be a Senator who shall not have attained to the age of thirty years, and been nine years a citizen of the United States, and who shall not, when elected, be an inhabitant of that State for which he shall be chosen.

The Vice-President of the United States shall be President of the Senate, but shall have no vote, unless they be equally divided.

The Senate shall choose their other officers and also a President *pro tempore* in the absence of the Vice-President, or when he shall exercise the office of President of the United States.

The Senate shall have the sole power to try all impeachments. When sitting for that purpose, they shall be on oath or affirmation. When the President of the United States is tried, the Chief Justice shall preside; and no person shall be convicted without the concurrence of two-thirds of the members present.

Judgment in cases of impeachment shall not extend further than to removal from office, and disqualification to hold and enjoy any office of honor, trust, or profit under the United States; but the party convicted shall, nevertheless, be liable and subject to indictment, trial, judgment, and punishment, according to law.

SECTION 4. The times, places, and manner of holding elections for Senators and Representatives shall be prescribed in each State by the legislature thereof; but the Congress may at any time by law make or alter such regulations, except as to the places of choosing Senators.

The Congress shall assemble at least once in every year, and such meeting shall be on the first Monday in December, unless they shall by law appoint a different day.

SECTION 5. Each House shall be the judge of the elections, returns, and qualifications of its own members, and a majority of each shall constitute a quorum to do business; but a smaller number may adjourn from day to day, and may be authorized to compel the attendance of absent members, in such manner, and under such penalties, as each House may provide. Each House may determine the rules of its proceedings, punish its members for disorderly behavior, and with the concurrence of two thirds, expel a member.

Each House shall keep a journal of its proceedings, and from time to time publish the same excepting such parts as may in their judgment require secrecy, and the yeas and nays of the members of either House on any question shall, at the desire of one-fifth of those present, be entered on the journal.

Neither House, during the session of Congress, shall, without the consent of the other, adjourn for more than three days, nor to any other place than that in which the two Houses shall be sitting.

SECTION 6. The Senators and Representatives shall receive a compensation for their services, to be ascertained by law and paid out of the Treasury of the United States. They shall, in all cases except treason, felony, and breach of the peace, be privileged from arrest during their attendance at the session of their respective Houses, and in going to and returning from the same; and for any speech or debate in either House, they shall not be questioned in any other place.

No Senator or Representative shall, during the time for which he was elected, be appointed to any civil office under the authority of the United States, which shall have been created, or the emoluments whereof shall have been increased during such time; and no person holding any office under the United States shall be a member of either House during his continuance in office.

SECTION 7. All bills for raising revenue shall originate in the House of Representatives; but the Senate may propose or concur with amendments as on other bills.

Every bill which shall have passed the House of Representatives and the Senate shall, before it become a law, be presented to the President of the United States; if he approve he shall sign it, but if not he shall return it, with his objections, to that House in which it shall have originated, who shall enter the objections at large on their journal and proceed to reconsider it. If after such reconsideration two-thirds of that House shall agree to pass the bill, it shall be sent, together with the objections, to the other House, by which it shall likewise be reconsidered, and if approved by two-thirds of that House it shall become a law. But in all such cases the vote of both Houses shall be determined by yeas and nays, and the names of the persons voting for and against the bill shall be entered on the journal of each House respectively. If any bill shall not be returned by the President within ten days (Sundays excepted) after it shall have been presented to him, the same shall be a law, in like manner as if he had signed it, unless the Congress by their adjournment prevent its return, in which case it shall not be a law.

Every order, resolution or vote to which the concurrence of the Senate and the House of Representatives may be necessary (except on a question of adjournment) shall be presented to the President of the United States; and before the same shall take effect, shall be approved by him, or being disapproved by him, shall be repassed by two-thirds of the Senate and House of

Representatives, according to the rules and limitations prescribed in the case of a bill.

SECTION 8. The Congress shall have power

To lay and collect taxes, duties, imposts and excises; to pay the debts and provide for the common defence and general welfare of the United States; but all duties, imposts, and excises, shall be uniform throughout the United States;

To borrow money on the credit of the United States;

To regulate commerce with foreign nations, and among the several States, and with the Indian tribes;

To establish an uniform rule of naturalization, and uniform laws on the subject of bankruptcies throughout the United States;

To coin money, regulate the value thereof, and of foreign coin, and fix the standard of weights and measures;

To provide for the punishment of counterfeiting the securities and current coin of the United States;

To establish post offices and post roads;

To promote the progress of science and useful arts by securing for limited times to authors and inventors the exclusive right to their respective writings and discoveries;

To constitute tribunals inferior to the Supreme Court;

To define and punish piracies and felonies committed on the high seas and offences against the law of nations;

To declare war, grant letters of marque and reprisal, and make rules concerning captures on land and water;

To raise and support armies, but no appropriation of money to that use shall be for a longer term than two years;

To provide and maintain a navy;

To make rules for the government and regulation of the land and naval forces;

To provide for calling forth the militia to execute the laws of the Union, suppress insurrections, and repel invasions;

To provide for organizing, arming, and disciplining the militia, and for governing such parts of them as may be employed in the service of the United States, reserving to the States respectively the appointment of the officers, and the authority of training the militia according to the discipline prescribed by Congress;

To exercise exclusive legislation in all cases whatsoever over such district (not exceeding ten miles square) as may, by cession of particular States and the acceptance of Congress, become the seat of the government of the United States, and to exercise like authority over all places purchased by the consent of the legislature of the State in which the same shall be, for the erection of forts, magazines, arsenals, dock yards, and other needful buildings;

To make all laws which shall be necessary and proper for carrying into execution the foregoing powers, and all other powers vested by this Constitution in the government of the United States, or in any department or officer thereof.

Section 9. The migration or importation of such persons as any of the States now existing shall think proper to admit shall not be prohibited by the Congress prior to the year one thousand eight hundred and eight, but a tax or duty may be imposed on such importation, not exceeding ten dollars for each person.

The privilege of the writ of *habeas corpus* shall not be suspended, unless when in cases of rebellion or invasion the public safety may require it.

No bill of attainder or *ex post facto* law shall be passed.

No capitation or other direct tax shall be laid, unless in proportion to the *census* or enumeration herein before directed to be taken.

No tax or duty shall be laid on articles exported from any State. No preference shall be given by any regulation of commerce or revenue to the ports of one State over those of another; nor shall vessels bound to or from one State be obliged to enter, clear or pay duties in another.

No money shall be drawn from the Treasury, but in consequence of appropriations made by law; and a regular statement and account of the receipts and expenditures of all public money shall be published from time to time.

No title of nobility shall be granted by the United States; and no person holding any office of profit or trust under them, shall, without the consent of the Congress accept of any present, emolument, office, or title of any kind whatever from any king, prince, or foreign state.

SECTION 10. No State shall enter into any treaty, alliance, or confederation; grant letters of marque and reprisal; coin money; emit bills of credit; make any thing but gold and silver coin a tender in payment of debts; pass any bill of attainder, *ex post facto* law, or law impairing the obligation of contracts, or grant any title of nobility.

No state shall, without the consent of the Congress, lay any imposts or duties on imports or exports, except what may be absolutely necessary for executing its inspection laws; and the net produce of all duties and imposts, laid by any State on imports or exports, shall be for the use of the Treasury of the United States; and all such laws shall be subject to the revision and control of the Congress. No State shall, without the consent of Congress, lay any duties of tonnage, keep troops and ships of war in time of peace, enter into any agreement or compact with another State, or with a foreign power, or engage in war, unless actually invaded, or in such imminent danger as will not admit of delay.

ARTICLE II. SECTION 1. The executive power shall be vested in a President of the United States of America. He shall hold his office during the term of four years, and together with the Vice-President, chosen for the same term, be elected as follows:

Each State shall appoint, in such manner as the legislature thereof may direct, a number of Electors, equal to the whole number of Senators and Representatives to which the State may be entitled in the Congress, but no Senator or Representative, or person holding an office of trust or profit under the United States, shall be appointed an Elector.

The Electors shall meet in their respective States and vote by ballot for two persons, of whom one at least shall not be an inhabitant of the same State with themselves. And they shall make a list of all the persons voted for, and of the number of votes for each; which list they shall sign and certify, and transmit sealed to the seat of government of the United States, directed to the President of the Senate. The President of the Senate shall, in the presence of the Senate and House of Representatives, open all the certificates, and the votes shall then be counted. The person having the greatest number of votes shall be the President, if such number be a majority of the whole number of electors appointed; and if there be more than one who have such majority, and have an equal number of votes, then the House of Representatives shall immediately choose by ballot one of them for President; and if no person have a majority, then from the five highest on the list the said House shall in like manner choose the President. But in choosing the President, the votes shall be taken by States, the representation from each State having one vote; a quorum for this purpose shall consist of a member or members from two-thirds of the States, and a majority of all the States shall be necessary to a choice. In every case, after the choice of the President, the person having the greatest number of votes of the Electors shall be the Vice-President. But if there should remain two or more who have equal votes, the Senate shall choose from them by ballot the Vice-President.

The Congress may determine the time of choosing the Electors, and the day on which they shall give their votes; which day shall be the same throughout the United States.

No person except a natural-born citizen, or citizen of the United States at the time of the adoption of this Constitution, shall be eligible to the office of President; neither shall any person be eligible to that office who shall not have attained to the age of thirty-five years, and been fourteen years a resident within the United States.

In case of the removal of the President from office, or of his death, resignation, or inability to discharge the powers and duties of the said office, the same shall devolve on the Vice-President, and the Congress may by law provide for the case of removal, death, resignation, or inability, both of the President and Vice-President, declaring what officer shall then act as President, and such officer shall act accordingly until the disability be removed or a President shall be elected.

The President shall, at stated times, receive for his services a compensation, which shall neither be increased nor diminished during the period for which he shall have been elected, and he shall not receive within that period any other emolument from the United States or any of them.

Before he enter on the execution of his office he shall take the following oath or affirmation:

"I do solemnly swear (or affirm) that I will faithfully execute the office of President of the United States, and will to the best of my ability, preserve, protect, and defend the Constitution of the United States."

SECTION 2. The President shall be Commander-in-Chief of the army and navy of the United States, and of the militia of the several States when called into the actual service of the United States; he may require the opinion, in writing, of the principal officer in each of the executive departments, upon any subject relating to the duties of their respective offices, and he shall have power to grant reprieves and pardons for offences against the United States, except in cases of impeachment.

He shall have power, by and with the advice and consent of the Senate, to make treaties, provided two thirds of the senators present concur; and he shall nominate, and, by and with the advice and consent of the Senate, shall appoint ambassadors, other public ministers and consuls, judges of the Supreme Court, and all other officers of the United States whose appointments are not herein otherwise provided for, and which shall be established by law; but the Congress may by law vest the appointment of such inferior officers, as they think proper, in the President alone, in the courts of law, or in the heads of departments.

The President shall have power to fill up all vacancies that may happen during the recess of the Senate, by granting commissions which shall expire at the end of their next session.

SECTION 3. He shall from time to time give to the Congress information of the state of the Union, and recommend to their consideration such measures as he shall judge necessary and expedient; he may, on extraordinary occasions, convene both Houses, or either of them, and in case of disagreement between them, with respect to the time of adjournment, he may adjourn them to such time as he shall think proper; he shall receive ambassadors and other public ministers; he shall take care that the laws be faithfully executed, and shall commission all the officers of the United States.

SECTION 4. The President, Vice-President and all civil officers of the United States shall be removed from office on impeachment for and conviction of treason, bribery, or other high crimes and misdemeanors.

ARTICLE III. SECTION 1. The judicial power of the United States shall be vested in one Supreme Court, and in such inferior courts as the Congress may from time to time ordain and establish. The judges, both of the supreme and inferior courts, shall hold their offices during good behavior, and shall, at stated times, receive for their services a compensation which shall not be diminished during their continuance in office.

SECTION 2. The Judicial power shall extend to all cases in law and equity, arising under this Constitution, the laws of the United States, and treaties made, or which shall be made, under their authority; to all cases affecting ambassadors, other public ministers, and consuls; to all cases of admiralty and maritime jurisdiction; to controversies to which the United States shall be a party; to controversies between two or more States; between a State and citizen of another State; between citizens of different States; between citizens of the same State claiming lands under grants of different States, and between a State, or the citizens thereof, and foreign states, citizens, or subjects.

In all cases affecting ambassadors, other public ministers and consuls, and those in which a State shall be party, the Supreme Court shall have original jurisdiction. In all the other cases before mentioned the Supreme Court shall have appellate jurisdiction, both as to law and fact, with such exceptions and under such regulations as the Congress shall make.

The trial of all crimes, except in cases of impeachment, shall be by jury; and such trial shall be held in the State where the said crimes shall have been committed; but when not committed within any State, the trial shall be at such place or places as the Congress may by law have directed.

SECTION 3. Treason against the United States shall consist only in levying war against them, or in adhering to their enemies, giving them aid and comfort. No person shall be convicted of treason unless on the testimony of two witnesses to the same overt act, or on confession in open court.

The Congress shall have power to declare the punishment of treason, but no attainder of treason shall work corruption of blood or forfeiture except during the life of the person attainted.

ARTICLE IV. SECTION 1. Full faith and credit shall be given in each State to the public acts, records, and judicial proceedings of every other State. And the Congress may by general laws prescribe the manner in which such acts, records, and proceedings shall be proved, and the effect thereof.

SECTION 2. The citizens of each State shall be entitled to all privileges and immunities of citizens in the several States.

A person charged in any State with treason, felony, or other crime, who shall flee from justice, and be found in another State, shall, on demand of the executive authority of the State from which he fled, be delivered up, to be removed to the State having jurisdiction of the crime.

No person held to service or labor in one State, under the laws thereof, escaping into another, shall, in consequence of any law or regulation therein, be discharged from such service or labor, but shall be delivered up on claim to the party to whom such service or labor may be due.

SECTION 3. New States may be admitted by the Congress into this Union; but no new State shall be formed or erected within the jurisdiction of any other State; nor any State be formed by the junction of two or more States, or parts of States, without the consent of the legislatures of the States concerned as well as of the Congress.

The Congress shall have power to dispose of and make all needful rules and regulations respecting the territory or other property belonging to the United States; and nothing in this Constitution shall be so construed as to prejudice any claims of the United States or any particular State.

SECTION 4. The United States shall guarantee to every State in this Union a republican form of government, and shall protect each of them against invasion, and on application of the legislature, or of the Executive (when the legislature cannot be convened), against domestic violence.

ARTICLE V. The Congress, whenever two thirds of both houses shall deem it necessary, shall propose amendments to this Constitution, or, on the application of the legislatures of two thirds of the several States, shall call a convention for proposing amendments, which in either case shall be valid to all intents and purposes as part of this Constitution, when ratified by the legislatures of three-fourths of the several States, or by conventions in three-fourths thereof, as the one or the other mode of ratification may be proposed by the Congress; provided, that no amendment which may be made prior to the year one thousand eight hundred and eight shall in any manner affect the first and fourth clauses in the Ninth Section of the First Article; and that no State, without its consent shall be deprived of its equal suffrage in the Senate.

ARTICLE VI. All debts contracted and engagements entered

into, before the adoption of this Constitution, shall be as valid against the United States under this Constitution as under the Confederation.

This Constitution, and the laws of the United States which shall be made in pursuance thereof, and all treaties made, or which shall be made, under the authority of the United States, shall be the supreme law of the land; and the judges in every State shall be bound thereby, any thing in the Constitution or laws of any State to the contrary notwithstanding.

The Senators and Representatives before mentioned, and the members of the several State legislatures, and all executive and judicial officers both of the United States and of the several States, shall be bound by oath or affirmation to support this Constitution; but no religious test shall ever be required as a qualification to any office or public trust under the United States.

ARTICLE VII. The ratification of the conventions of nine States shall be sufficient for the establishment of this Constitution between the States so ratifying the same.

DONE in convention, by the unanimous consent of the States present, the seventeenth day of September, in the year of our Lord one thousand seven hundred and eighty-seven, and of the independence of the United States of America the twelfth. In witness whereof, we have hereunto subscribed our names.

GEORGE WASHINGTON, *President, Deputy from Virginia.*

New-Hampshire:
John Langdon
Nicholas Gilman

Massachusetts:
Nathaniel Gorham
Rufus King

Connecticut:
William Samuel Johnson
Roger Sherman

New York:
Alexander Hamilton

New Jersey:
William Livingston
David Brearley
William Paterson
Jonathan Dayton

Pennsylvania:
Benjamin Franklin
Thomas Mifflin
Robert Morris
George Clymer
Thomas Fitzsimons
Jared Ingersoll
James Wilson
Gouverneur Morris

Delaware:
George Read
Gunning Bedford, *Junior*
John Dickinson
Richard Bassett
Jacob Broom

Maryland:
James M'Henry
Daniel Jenifer, *of St. Thomas*
Daniel Carroll

Virginia:
John Blair
James Madison, *Junior*

North Carolina:
William Blount
Richard Dobbs Spaight
Hugh Williamson

South Carolina:
John Rutledge
Charles Cotesworth Pinckney
Charles Pinckney
Pierce Butler

Georgia:
William Few
Abraham Baldwin

Attest. WILLIAM JACKSON, *Secretary*

IV

THE
FEDERALIST
ARGUMENTS

The classic discussion of the Constitution is still *The Federalist,* a series of newspaper essays written by Hamilton, Madison, and John Jay to support the cause of ratification by the state conventions, especially in New York. The papers were published during a period of several months over the signature "Publius." Such pen names were common during the period. Other comments on the Constitution were signed "Cato" or "Junius" or simply "a farmer."

These brief excerpts from *The Federalist* should be read, of course, with the preceding material in mind. They are included for many reasons, primarily because they shed light on the Constitution itself and on the reasons why men such as Hamilton and Madison thought its adoption was so important. Like everything else in this unit this section should also help you to understand the Constitution, not as a document descended from heaven, but as a consequence of a particular time and the efforts of particular men.

A. It has often given me pleasure to observe, that independent America was not composed of detached and distant territories, but that one connected, fertile, wide-spreading country was the portion of our western sons of liberty. Providence has in a particular manner blessed it with a variety of soils and productions, and watered it with innumerable streams, for the delight and accommodation of its inhabitants. A succession of navigable waters forms a kind of chain round its borders, as if to bind it together; while the most noble rivers in the world, running at convenient distances, present them with highways for the easy communication of friendly aids, and the mutual transportation and exchange of their various commodities.

With equal pleasure I have as often taken notice, that Providence has been pleased to give this one connected country to one united people—a people descended from the same ancestors, speaking the same language, professing the same religion, attached to the same principles of government, very similar in their manners and customs, and who, by their joint counsels, arms and efforts, fighting side by side throughout a long and bloody war, have nobly established general liberty and independence.

This country and this people seem to have been made for each other, and it appears as if it was the design of Providence, that an inheritance so proper and convenient for a band of brethren, united to each other by the strongest ties, should never be split into a number of unsocial, jealous, and alien sovereignties.

John Jay in *The Federalist* #2.

B. [A]* The necessity of a Constitution, at least equally energetic with the one proposed, to the preservation of the Union, is the point at the examination of which we are now arrived.

* Bracketed initials added by Editor.

[B] Whether there ought to be a federal government in-trusted with the care of the common defense, is a question . . . open for discussion; but the moment it is decided in the affirmative, it will follow, that that government ought to be clothed with all the powers requisite to complete execution of its trust.

[C] Defective as the present Confederation has been proved to be, this principle appears to have been fully recognized by the framers of it; though they have not made proper or adequate provision for its exercise. Congress have an unlimited discretion to make requisitions of men and money; to govern the army and navy; to direct their operations. As their requisitions are made constitutionally binding upon the States, who are in fact under the most solemn obligations to furnish the supplies required of them, the intention evidently was, that the United States should command whatever resources were by them judged requisite to the "common defence and general welfare." It was presumed that a sense of their true interests, and a regard to the dictates of good faith, would be found sufficient pledges of the punctual performance of the duty of the members of the federal head.

[D] The experiment has, however, demonstrated that this expectation was ill-founded and illusory; and the observations, made under the last head, will, I imagine, have sufficed to convince the impartial and discerning, that there is an absolute necessity for an entire change in the first principles of the system; that if we are in earnest about giving the Union energy and duration, we must abandon the vain project of legislating upon the States in their collective capacities; we must extend the laws of the federal government to the individual citizens of America; we must discard the fallacious scheme of quotas and requisitions, as equally impracticable and unjust. The result from all this is that the Union ought to be invested with full power to levy troops; to build and equip fleets; and to raise the revenues which will be required for the formation and support of an army and navy, in the customary and ordinary modes practised in other governments.

[E] If the circumstances of our country are such as to demand a compound instead of a simple, a confederate instead of a sole, government, the essential point which will remain to be adjusted will be to discriminate the *objects,* as far as it can be done, which shall appertain to the different provinces or departments of power; allowing to each the most ample authority for fulfilling the objects committed to its charge. Shall the Union be constituted the guardian of the common safety? Are fleets and armies and revenues necessary to this purpose? The government of the Union must be empowered to pass all laws, and to make all regulations which have relation to them. The same must be the case in respect to commerce, and to every other matter to which its jurisdiction is permitted to extend. Is the administration of justice between the citizens of the same State the proper department of the local governments? These must possess all the authorities which are connected with this object, and with every other that may be allotted to their particular cognizance and direction. Not to confer in each case a degree of power commensurate to the end, would be to violate the most obvious rules of prudence and propriety, and improvidently to trust the great interests of the nation to hands which are disabled from managing them with vigor and success.

Who so likely to make suitable provisions for the public defence, as that body to which the guardianship of the public safety is confided; which, as the centre of information, will best understand the extent and urgency of the dangers that threaten; as the representative of the *Whole,* will feel itself most deeply interested in the preservation of every part; which, from the responsibility implied in the duty assigned to it, will be most sensibly impressed with the necessity of proper exertions; and which, by the extension of its authority throughout the States, can alone establish uniformity and concert in the plans and measures by which the common safety is to be secured? Is there not a manifest inconsistency in devolving upon the federal government the care of the general defence, and leaving in the State governments the *effective* powers by which it is to be provided for? Is not a want of co-operation the infallible consequence of such a system? And will not weakness, disorder, and undue distribution of the burdens and calamities of war, an unnecessary and intolerable increase of expense, be its natural and inevitable concomitants? Have we not had unequivocal experience of its effects in the course of the revolution which we have just accomplished?

[F] Every view we may take of the subject, as candid inquirers after truth, will serve to convince us, that it is both unwise and dangerous to deny the federal government an unconfined authority, as to all those objects which are intrusted to its management. It will indeed deserve the most vigilant and careful attention of the people, to see that it be modelled in such a manner as to admit of its being safely vested with the requisite powers. If any plan which has been, or may be, offered to our consideration, should not, upon a dispassionate inspection, be found to answer this description, it ought to be rejected. A government, the constitution of which renders it unfit to be trusted with all the powers which a free people ought to delegate to any government, would be an unsafe and an improper depository of the *National Interests*. Wherever *these* can with propriety be confided, the coincident powers may safely accompany them. This is the true result of all just reasoning upon the subject. And the adversaries of the plan promulgated by the convention ought to have confined themselves to showing, that the internal structure of the proposed government was such as to render it unworthy of the confidence of the people. They ought not to have wandered into inflammatory declamations and unmeaning cavils about the extent of the powers. The *powers* are not too extensive for the *objects* of federal administration, or, in other words, for the management of our NATIONAL INTERESTS: nor can any satisfactory argument be framed to show that they are chargeable with such an excess. If it be true, as has been insinuated by some of the writers on the other side, that the difficulty arises from the nature of the thing, and that the extent of the country will not permit us to form a government in which such ample powers can safely be reposed, it would prove that we ought to contract our views, and resort to the expedient of separate confederacies, which will move within more practicable spheres. For the absurdity must continually stare us in the face of confiding to a government the direction of the most essential national interests, without daring to trust it to the authorities which are indispensable to their proper and efficient management. Let us not attempt to reconcile contradictions, but firmly embrace a rational alternative.

Hamilton in *The Federalist* #23 (1788).

G. In the compound republic of America, the power surrendered by the people is first divided between two distinct governments, and then the portion allotted to each subdivided among distinct and separate departments. Hence a double security arises to the rights of the people. The different governments will control each other, at the same time that each will be controlled by itself.

Hamilton or Madison in *The Federalist* #51 (1788).

V

THE
ANTI–FEDERALISTS

Support of the Constitution was by no means universal. Indeed there is evidence that most Americans were apathetic. Many, moreover, were actively opposed. You might ask yourself not only the reasons for their opposition, but you also may wish to think back to previous American history to find the particular events and experiences that might provoke opposition. Perhaps it would also be fruitful to see, in a tentative way, not only how the anti-Federalists differed from the Federalists, but whether they agreed on anything. Among the leaders of the anti-Federalists, those who opposed the Constitution were three prominent Virginians, Patrick Henry, Richard Henry Lee, and George Mason. Other notable opponents were Governor George Clinton of New York, Sam Adams of Massachusetts (who later changed his views) and Luther Martin of Maryland.

A. This Constitution is said to have beautiful features: but when I came to examine these features, sir, they appear to me horribly frightful. Among other deformities, it has an awful squinting; it squints toward monarchy; and does not this raise indignation in the breast of every true American?

Your President may easily become king. Your senate is so imperfectly constructed that your dearest rights may be sacrificed by what may be a small minority; and a very small minority may continue forever unchangeably this government, although horridly defective. Where are your checks in this government? Your strongholds will be in the hands of your enemies. It is on a supposition that your American governors shall be honest, that all the good qualities of this government are founded; but its defective and imperfect construction puts it in their power to perpetrate the worst of mischiefs, should they be bad men; and, sir, would not all the world, from the eastern to the western hemisphere, blame our distracted folly in resting our rights upon the contingency of our rulers being good or bad? Show me that age and country where the rights and liberties of the people were placed on the sole chance of their rulers being good men, without a consequent loss of liberty! I say that the loss of that dearest privilege has ever followed, with absolute certainty, every such mad attempt.

If your American chief be a man of ambition and abilities, how easy it is for him to render himself absolute! The army is in his hands, and if he be a man of address, it will be attached to him, and it will be the subject of long meditation with him to seize the first auspicious moment to accomplish his design; and, sir, will the American spirit solely relieve you when this happens? I would rather infinitely—and I am sure most of this Convention are of the same opinion—have a king, lords, and commons, than a government so replete with such insupportable evils. If we make a king, we may prescribe the rules by which he shall rule his people, and interpose such checks as shall prevent him from infringing them; but the President, in the field at the head of his army, can prescribe the terms on which he shall reign master, so far that it will puzzle any American ever to get his neck from under the galling yoke. I cannot with patience think of this idea. If ever he violates the laws, one of two things will happen: he will come at the head of his army, to carry every thing before him; or he will give bail, or do what Mr. Chief Justice will order him. If he be guilty, will not the recollection of his crimes teach him to make one bold push for the American throne? Will not the immense difference between being master of every thing, and being ignominiously tried and punished, powerfully excite him to make this bold push? But, sir, where is the existing force to punish him? Can he not, at the head of his army, beat down every opposition? Away with your President! we shall have a king; the army will salute him monarch: your militia will leave you, and assist in making him king, and fight against you: and what have you to oppose this force? What will then become of you and your rights? Will not absolute despotism ensue?

(Here Mr. Henry strongly and pathetically expatiated on the probability of the President's enslaving America, and the horrid consequences that must result.)

What can be more defective than the clause concerning the elections? The control given to Congress over the time, place, and manner of holding elections, will totally destroy the end of suffrage. The elections may be held at one place, and the most inconvenient in the state; or they may be at remote distances from those who have a right of suffrage; hence nine out of ten must either not vote at all, or vote for strangers; for the most influential characters will be applied to, to know who are the most proper to be chosen. I repeat, that the control of Congress over the *manner*, &c., of electing well warrants this idea. The natural consequence will be, that this democratic branch will possess none of the public confidence; the people will be prejudiced against representatives chosen in such an injudicious manner. The proceedings in the northern conclave will be hidden from the yeomanry of this country. We are told that the yeas and nays shall be taken, and entered on the journals. This, sir, will avail nothing: it may be locked up in their chests, and concealed forever from the people; for they are not to publish what parts they think require secrecy: they *may* think, and *will think,* the whole requires it. Another beautiful feature of this Constitution is the publication from time to time of the receipts and expenditures of the public money.

This expression, *from time to time,* is very indefinite and indeterminate: it may extend to a century. Grant that any of them are wicked; they may squander the public money so as to ruin you, and yet this expression will give you no redress. I say they may ruin you; for where, sir, is the responsibility? The yeas and nays will show you nothing, unless they be fools as well as knaves; for, after having wickedly trampled on the rights of the people, they would act like fools indeed, were they to publish and divulge their iniquity, when they have it equally in their power to suppress and conceal it. Where is the responsibility—that leading principle in British government? In that government, a punishment certain and inevitable is provided; but in this, there is no real, actual punishment for the grossest mal-administration. They may go without punishment, though they commit the most outrageous violation on our immunities. That paper may tell me they will be punished. I ask, By what law? They must make a law, for there is not law existing to do it. What! Will they make a law to punish themselves?

This, sir, is my greatest objection to the Constitution, that there is no true responsibility—and that the preservation of our liberty depends on the single chance of men being virtuous enough to make laws to punish themselves.

Patrick Henry in the Virginia Ratifying Convention, June 1788.

B. . . . Dr. Smith . . . pressed the question upon Henry, why he had not taken his seat in the (Philadelphia) Convention and lent his aid in making a good Constitution, instead of staying at home and abusing the work of his patriotic compeers? Henry . . . replied "I smelt a Rat."*

H. B. Grigsby, *History of the Virginia Federal Convention of 1788.*

C. There is no declaration of rights: (a bill of rights for individuals and states) and the laws of the general government being paramount to the laws and constitutions of the several states, the declarations of rights in the separate states are no security.

George Mason (a member of the Philadelphia Convention who had refused to sign), Letter to Washington, October 18, 1787.

D. We are now fixing a national consolidation. This section . . . is big with mischiefs. Congress will have power to keep standing armies. The great Mr. Pitt says, standing armies are dangerous . . . keep your militia in order—we don't want standing armies. A gentleman said, We are a rich state: I say so too. Then why shall we not wait five or six months, and see what our sister states do?

We are able to stand our ground against a foreign power; they cannot starve us out; they cannot bring their ships on the land; we are a nation of healthy and strong men; our land is fertile** . . .

* Henry had been chosen by Virginia but refused to go.

** This was a reference to Article VI. After nine states ratified, the other four would either have to do so also or operate as independent nations.

Let us amend the old Confederation. Why not give Congress power only to regulate trade? . . . Why all this racket? Gentlemen say we are undone if we cannot stop up the Thames; but nations will mind their own interest, and not ours. Great Britain has found the secret to pick the subjects' pockets, without their knowing of it; that is the very thing Congress is after . . . where is the bill of rights which shall check the power of this Congress; which shall say, *Thus far shall ye come, and no farther.*

A delegate in the Massachusetts ratifying convention, 1788.

E. The corrupting nature of power, and its insatiable appetite for increase, hath proved the necessity, and procured the adoption of the strongest and most express declarations of that *Residuum* of natural rights, which is not intended to be given up to Society; and which indeed is not necessary to be given for any good social purpose. In a government therefore, when the power of judging what shall be for the *general welfare,* which goes to every object of human legislation; and where the laws of such Judges shall be the *supreme Law of the Land*: it seems to be of the last consequence to declare in most explicit terms the reservations above alluded to. So much for the propriety of a Bill of Rights as a necessary bottom to this new system—It is in vain to say that the defects in this new Constitution may be remedied by the Legislature created by it. . . . Surely this is not a ground upon which a wise and good man would choose to rest the dearest rights of human nature. Indeed, some capital defects are not within the compass of legislative redress—The Oligarchic tendency from the combination of President, V. President, &

Senate, is a ruin not within legislative remedy. Nor is the partial right of voting in the Senate, or the defective numbers in the house of Representatives. It is of little consequence to say that the numbers in the last mentioned Assembly will increase with the population of these States, because what may happen in twenty five or 27 years hence is poor alleviation of the evil, that the immediate time is big with; for it often happens that abuse under the name of Use is rivetted upon Mankind. Nor can a good reason be assigned for establishing a bad, instead of a good government, in the first instance, because time may amend the bad—Men do not choose to be sick because it may happen that physic may cure them—Suppose that good men came first to the administration of this government; and that they should see, or think they see, a necessity for trying criminally a Man without giving him his Jury of the Vicinage; or that the freedom of the Press should be restrained because it disturbed the operations of the new government—the mutilation of the jury trial, and the restraint of the press would then follow for good purposes as it should seem, and by good men—But these precedents will be followed by bad men to sacrifice honest and innocent men; and to suppress the exertions of the Press for wicked and tyrannic purposes . . . In proof of this, we know that the wise and good Lord Holt, to support King William and Revolution principles, produced doctrines in a case of Libel (King against Bear) subversive both of law and sound sense; which his successor Lord Mansfield (in the case of Woodfall) would have availed himself of for the restraint of the Press and the ruin of liberty. It would appear therefore, that the consideration of human perversity renders it necessary for human safety that in the first place, power not requisite should not be given, and in the next place that necessary powers should be carefully guarded. How far this is done in the New Constitution I submit to your wise and attentive consideration. Whether, for the present, it may not be sufficient so to alter the Confederation as to allow Congress full liberty to make Treaties by removing the restraining clauses; by giving the Impost for a limited time, and the power of Regulating trade; is a question that deserves to be considered.

But I think the new Constitution (properly amended) as it contains many good regulations, may be admitted—And why not such indispensable amendments be proposed by the Conventions and returned with the new plan to Congress that a new general Convention may so weave them into the proffer'd system as that a Web may be produced fit for freemen to wear? If such amendments were proposed by a Capital state or two, & a willingness expressed to agree with the plan so amended; I cannot see why it may not be affected. It is a mere begging the question to suppose, as some do, that only this moment and this measure will do. But, Why so, there being no war external or internal to prevent due deliberation on this momentous business—The public papers will inform you what violence has been practised by the Agitators of this new System in Philadelphia to drive on to its immediate adoption as if the subject of Government were a business of passion, instead of cool, sober, and intense consideration.* I shall not leave this place before the 4th of November—in the mean time I shall be happy to hear from you—My best compliments are presented to Mrs. Adams, and I pray to be remembered to Gen. Warren, Mr. Lovell & the good Doctor Holten when you see him. I am, with sentiments of the truest esteem & regard dear Sir your affectionate friend.

Richard Henry Lee to Samuel Adams, October 5, 1787.

* This a reference to events discussed in the next section (VI) of this booklet.

"Publius" and other Federalists took pains to refute the arguments for a bill of rights.

F. I go further, and affirm that bills of rights, in the sense and to the extent in which they are contended for, are not only unnecessary in the proposed Constitution, but would even be dangerous. They would contain various exceptions to powers not granted; and, on this very account would afford a colorable pretext to claim more than were granted. For why declare that things shall not be done which there is no power to do? Why, for instance, should it be said that the liberty of the press shall not be restrained, when no power is given by which restrictions may be imposed? I will not contend that such a provision would confer a regulating power; but it is evident that it would furnish, to men disposed to usurp, a plausible pretence for claiming that power. They might urge with a semblance of reason, that the Constitution ought not to be charged with the absurdity of providing against the abuse of an authority which was not given, and that the provision against restraining the liberty of the press afforded a clear implication, that a power to prescribe proper regulations concerning it was intended to be vested in the national government. This may serve as a specimen of the numerous handles which would be given to the doctrine of constructive powers, by the indulgence of an injudicious zeal for bills of rights.

On the subject of the liberty of the press, as much as has been said, I cannot forbear adding a remark or two: in the first place, I observe, that there is not a syllable concerning it in the constitution of this State; in the next, I contend, that whatever has been said about it in that of any other State, amounts to nothing. What signifies a declaration, that "the liberty of the press shall be inviolably preserved?" What is the liberty of the press? Who can give it any definition which would not leave the utmost latitude for evasion? I hold it to be impracticable; and from this I infer, that its security, whatever fine declarations may be inserted in any constitution respecting it, must altogether depend on public opinion, and on the general spirit of the people and of the government.* And here, after all, as is intimated upon another occasion, must we seek for the only solid basis of all our rights.

There remains but one other view of this matter to conclude the point. The truth is, after all the declamations we have heard, that the Constitution is itself, in every rational sense, and to every useful purpose, A BILL OF RIGHTS. The several bills of rights in Great Britain form its Constitution, and conversely the constitution of each State is its bill of rights. And the proposed Constitution, if adopted, will be the bill of rights of the Union. Is it one object of a bill of rights to declare and specify the political privileges of the citizens in the structure and administration

* To show that there is a power in the Constitution by which the liberty of the press may be affected, recourse has been had to the power of taxation. It is said that duties may be laid upon the publications so high as to amount to a prohibition. I know not by what logic it could be maintained, that the declarations in the State constitutions, in favor of the freedom of the press, would be a constitutional impediment to the imposition of duties upon publications by the State legislatures. It cannot certainly be pretended that any degree of duties, however low, would be an abridgement of the liberty of the press. We know that newspapers are taxed in Great Britain, and yet it is notorious that the press nowhere enjoys greater liberty than in that country. And if duties of any kind may be laid without a violation of that liberty, it is evident that the extent must depend on legislative discretion, regulated by public opinion; so that, after all, general declarations respecting the liberty of the press, will give it no greater security than it will have without them. The same invasions of it may be effected under the State constitutions which contain those declarations through the means of taxation as under the proposed Constitution, which has nothing of the kind. It would be quite as significant to declare that government ought to be free, that taxes ought not to be excessive, etc., as that the liberty of the press ought not to be restrained.

— PUBLIUS

of the government? This is done in the most ample and precise manner in the plan of the convention; comprehending various precautions for the public security, which are not to be found in any of the State constitutions. Is another object of a bill of rights to define certain immunities and modes of proceeding, which are relative to personal and private concerns? This we have seen has also been attended to, in a variety of cases, in the same plan. Advertising therefore to the substantial meaning of a bill of rights, it is absurd to allege that it is not to be found in the work of the convention. It may be said that it does not go far enough, though it will not be easy to make this appear; but it can with no propriety be contended that there is no such thing. It certainly must be immaterial what mode is observed as to the order of declaring the rights of the citizens, if they are to be found in any part of the instrument which establishes the government. And hence it must be apparent, that much of what has been said on this subject rests merely on verbal and nominal distinctions, entirely foreign from the substance of the thing.

Hamilton in *The Federalist* #84, 1788.

VI

RATIFICATION

(Before proceeding with this section, be sure you are familiar with the chronology in Appendix A at the end of this booklet.)

Much of the reading in this section is light. It is to give you a little more of an idea that Americans of 1787–88 were not plastercast abstractions or demigods always engaged in sedate drawing room deliberations. But there is also another purpose for this section. It is always the object of the historian to order, to organize, to find reasons. It was, in some states, the act of ratification itself that provided the articulate and forceful demands for modification. In short, the ratifying conventions helped set the scene for the next episode.

In some states ratification was overwhelming and rapid. Among them were New Jersey, Georgia, Delaware, Connecticut. But in some of the large states, notably New York and Virginia, the issue remained in doubt until the very end of the ratifying convention. North Carolina failed to approve at its first convention and Rhode Island did not even hold one until the new government had begun to function.

In Pennsylvania, the Assembly, dominated by a Federalist majority, made attempts to call a ratifying convention as quickly as possible. The opponents of the Constitution, fearing they would be outvoted, tried delaying tactics. Many of them refused to attend the sessions in order to prevent a quorum.

A. (A Federalist crowd) . . . broke into their lodgings, seized them, dragged them through the streets to the State House, and thrust them into the assembly room, with clothes torn and faces white with rage. The quorum was now complete.

McMaster and Stone, *Pennsylvania and the Federal Constitution*, 1888.

B. About midnight on Tuesday last, a great concourse of people assembled opposite to the house of Mr. Alexander Boyd (where the anti-Federalists stayed). The persons thus assembled made a considerable noise in the streets, and at length assailed Mr. Boyd's house, beating loudly at the door, and breaking the windows, through which they threw some very large stones, etc., exclaiming repeatedly, "here the damned rascals live who did all the mischief," and using other words highly reproachful to the members of this house and of the executive council.

An anti-Federalist, James McLean, in the Pennsylvania assembly, 1787. (This is not a reference to the same incident described above.)

C. On Wednesday, the 26th of December last, a number of persons here, much in love with the new Constitution, formed a plan of rejoicing on account of the adoption by this State; they kept their purpose a profound secret from the rest of the inhabitants (who they knew were of a different opinion) until near night, at which time a cannon was brought from the public magazine, placed in the centre of the square, a drum beat and the bell rung; this collected a vast concourse of people, and a report having been propagated that whoever did not illuminate their windows would have them broke in pieces. This alarmed the people very much, who asked the rejoicers what they intended, and why they placed a cannon there at that time; they answered, it was to express their approbation of the adoption of the federal Constitution; they were then asked why they attempted to do so without calling a town meeting, to take the sense of the people on the subject. They replied that such as did not like it might let it alone— that they were determined, in spite of all opposition, to fire that cannon, and swearing most tremendously, if they would not clear the way, they would fire it through their bodies. A smart altercation now took place between both parties, when a number of barrels which had been piled for the bonfire, were thrown down; this provoked some of the most violent of the rejoicers to lay about them most unmercifully with such weapons as they were provided with, but the people defended themselves so well, and aimed their blows so successfully, that it soon converted the intended joy into mourning—the most forward of the rejoicing party were either carried off, or ran with the greatest precipitation, not caring longer to face the hardy cuffs of their enraged opponents, who they knew would pay no respect to their rank, nor make any allowance for their delicate constitutions; I assure you it was laughable to see lawyers, doctors, colonels, captains, etc., leave the scene of their rejoicing in such haste, and run some one way and some another, so that in about three minutes from the first commencement of the battle, there was not one of the rejoicing party to be seen on the ground, except a few who skulked in the dark, in order to collect what they could hear, with a view of appearing as evidences on a future day.

When the fray was over, the rejoicing took a new turn; the fragments of the broken barrels were collected, piled and set fire to; the new constitution was then produced and committed to the flames, by the hands of the executor of the law, amidst the loudest acclamations, then followed three cheers in honor of the dissenting minority of twenty-three in the State convention. Immediately after this (the people having mostly dispersed) some fellows whom the rejoicers had employed to assist them in working the cannon (but who deserted their cause when they saw them defeated) went so far as to burn the carriage and every part of the cannon-mounting that would burn, contrary to the express prohibition of such of the people as were then present, but now too few to prevent the rabble, at the head of whom was one Ryan, a late wheelbarrow convict, whom the rejoicers had employed to work the cannon for them; he swore (when desired to desist and not destroy the carriage) that first he would burn one side of the cannon, and then turn it like a po-ta-tee, for he was captain now.

Next day at noon the rejoicers collected a number of men with fire-arms and ammunition, in order (as they expressed it) to rejoice at the risk of their lives; they fired a few rounds, but on hearing the people's drum beat to arms, they dispersed, appointing to meet at two o'clock, to finish their rejoicings; this, however, they prudently declined. Now in their turn the people met, and having dressed up the effigies of two of the most noted partisans and promotors of the new constitution, after carrying them in procession through the principal streets of the town, to the funeral pile which was burning in the square for their reception, committed them to the flames, with an indignation suitable to the opinion they entertained of men who could endeavor to undermine the liberties of their country. From the first appearance of the effigies the dead bell tolled until they were totally consumed to ashes: This ended the exercises of the day; however the lawyers are like to make something of the matter—the rejoicers swear they will be avenged, they have summoned a long train of evidences before a justice who they think favors their party, and are endeavoring to injure a number of respectable characters among the people; who in their turn have it amply in their power to retaliate, but will only act agreeably to the laws of their country, the nod of the great not being yet the supreme law of the land.

ONE OF THE PEOPLE

Letter to a Pennsylvania Newspaper, January 1, 1788.

As far as is known, the proceedings in most other states were orderly although there is evidence of considerable political maneuvering in every convention in which the outcome was in doubt. In Massachusetts, it was reported, the Federalists swung over John Hancock with an implied promise for support to the post of vice-president. Rhode Island, the last state to ratify, acted in part under the spur of a threat by Providence and other towns to secede if the Constitution were not adopted there. However this threat did not materialize until the new U. S. government had organized and had become, in some senses, a foreign country to Rhode Island. Many of the framers, incidentally, were members of the new government.

To the Six Pillars of the Federal Edifice . . .

Toast at a formal dinner, Boston, May 1, 1788.

D. At the head of the hall were seven pillars of wreaths, decorated with flowers, emblematic of the seven states which have adopted the federal Constitution . . . on the keystones of the arches were painted the names of the states.

Report on the annual dinner of the "Ancient and Honorable Artillery Company of Boston" in the *Massachusetts Independent Chronicle*, June 5, 1788.

E. *Eleven Stars,* in quick succession rise—
   Eleven Columns strike our wondering eyes,
   Soon o'er the whole shall dwell the beauteous dome,
   Columbia's boasts and *Freedom's* hallow'd home.
   Here shall the arts in glorious splendor shine!
   And *Agriculture* give her stores divine!
   Commerce refin'd, dispense us more than gold—
   And this new world teach wisdom to the old—
   Religion here shall fix her blest abode,
   Arrayed in mildness, like its parent *God!*
   Justice and *Law* shall endless *Peace* maintain,
   And the *Saturnian Age* return again.

Massachusetts Centinel, August 1788, "On the Erection of the Eleventh Pillar of the Great National Dome."

F. (The Constitution is) a refuge in the howling wilderness of an almost national anarchy where were pits, scorpions and firey flying serpents.

A New England minister, 1791.

G. Had the government been formed on principles truly federal, as I wished it, legislating over and acting upon the states only in their collective or political capacity, and not on individuals, there would have been no need for a bill of rights . . . But the proposed Constitution being intended and empowered to act not only on states, but also immediately upon individuals, it renders a recognition and a stipulation in favor of the rights both of states and of men not only proper but, in my opinion, absolutely necessary.

Luther Martin, a member of the Philadelphia Convention who opposed the Constitution, March, 1788.

H. My head, my hand and my heart, shall be at liberty to retrieve the loss of liberty, and remove the defects of that system in a constitutional way. I wish not to go to violence, but will wait with hopes that the spirit which predominated in the revolution is not yet gone, nor the cause of those who are attached to the revolution yet lost. I shall therefore patiently wait in expectation of seeing that government changed.

Patrick Henry at the close of the Virginia Convention when the outcome was no longer in doubt, 1788.

I. (Henry) appears to be involved in gloomy mystery. Something surely is meditated against the new constitution, more animated, forcible and violent, than a simple application for a new convention.

Edmund Pendleton of Virginia to Madison, 1789.

J. It is the opinion of this Convention, that certain amendments and alterations in the said Constitution would remove the fears and quiet the apprehensions of many of the good people of the commonwealth . . . the Convention do therefore recommend that the following alterations and provisions be introduced into the said Constitution:

That it be explicitly declared, that all powers not expressly delegated by the aforesaid Constitution are reserved to the several States . . .

That Congress do not lay direct taxes, but when the moneys arising from the impost and excise are insufficient for the public exigencies . . .

That Congress erect no company with exclusive advantages of commerce . . .

From Resolution accompanying the ratification of the Constitution in the Massachusetts Convention.

K. We, the delegates of the people of Virginia, duly elected in pursuance of a recommendation from the General Assembly, and now met in Convention, having fully and freely investigated and discussed the proceedings of the federal Convention, and being prepared, as well as the most mature deliberation hath enabled us, to decide thereon, Do, in the name and in behalf of the people of Virginia, declare and make known, that the powers granted under the Constitution, being derived from the people of the United States, be resumed by them whensoever the same shall be perverted to their injury or oppression, and that *every* power, *not granted thereby, remains with them, and at their will;* that, therefore, no right, of any denomination, can be cancelled, abridged, restrained, or modified, by the Congress, by the Senate or House of Representatives, acting in any capacity, by the President, or any department or officer of the United States, except in those instances in which power is given by the Constitution for those purposes; and that, among other essential rights, the liberty of conscience and of the press cannot be cancelled, abridged, restrained, or modified, by any authority of the United States.

That there be a declaration or bill of rights asserting, and securing from encroachment, the essential and unalienable rights of the people, in some such manner as the following:

1st. That there are certain natural rights, of which men, when they form a social compact, cannot deprive or divest their posterity; among which are the enjoyment of life and liberty, with the means of acquiring, possessing and protecting property, and pursuing and obtaining happiness and safety.

2nd.   That all power is naturally invested in, and consequently derived from the people; that magistrates therefore are their *trustees* and *agents,* at all times amenable to them.

3rd.   That government ought to be instituted for the common benefit, protection, and security of the people; and that the doctrine of non-resistance against arbitrary power and oppression is absurd, slavish, and destructive to the good and happiness of mankind.

4th.   That no man or set of men are entitled to separate or exclusive public emoluments or privileges from the community, but in consideration of public services, which not being descendible, neither ought the offices of magistrate, legislator, or judge, or any other public office, to be hereditary . . .

That each state in the Union shall respectively retain every power, jurisdiction, and right, which is not by this Constitution delegated to the Congress of the United States . . .

That no person shall be capable of being President of the United States more than eight years in any term of sixteen years . . .

That Congress shall not alter, modify or interfere in the times, places or manner of holding elections for senators and representatives . . .

Excerpts from resolutions accompanying Virginia's ratification of the Constitution, 1788.

L. There have been objections of various kinds . . . against the Constitution, but I believe the great mass of the people who opposed it, disliked it because it did not contain effectual (guarantees against) encroachments on particular rights, and those safeguards which they have been long accustomed to have interposed between them and the magistrate who exercises the sovereign power; nor ought we to consider them safe, while a great number of our fellow citizens think these securities necessary.

Representative James Madison in the First Congress, 1789.

We see a great body of our constituents opposed to the Constitution as it now stands, who are apprehensive of the enormous powers of government. But if . . . it is thought proper to make amendments, it will remove this difficulty.

Representative Elbridge Gerry of Massachusetts in the First Congress, 1789.

N. Should we propose amendments North Carolina would accede (to the Constitution). It is doubtful in case we should not.

Representative Fisher Ames of Massachusetts in the First Congress, 1789.

O. The more I consider the subject of amendments, the more I am convinced it is improper . . . I am against inserting a declaration of rights in the Constitution . . . If such an addition is not dangerous or improper, it is at least unnecessary . . . Let me ask . . . what reason there is for the suspicions which are to be removed by this measure? Who are Congress, that such apprehensions should be entertained of them? Do we not belong to the mass of the people? Is there a single right that, if infringed, will not affect us and our connexions as much as any other person? . . . do gentlemen suppose bills of rights necessary to secure liberty? If they do, let them look at New York, New Jersey, Virginia, South Carolina and Georgia. Those States have no bills of rights and is the liberty of the citizens less safe . . . ?

Representative James Jackson of Georgia in the First Congress, June 1789.

P. I do not expect . . . perfection on this side of the grave in the works of man; but my opinion is, that we are not at present in circumstances to make (the Constitution) better. It is a wonder that there has been such unanimity in adopting it, considering the ordeal it had to undergo; and the unanimity which prevailed at its formation is equally astonishing . . . It seems to be the opinion of gentlemen (in Congress) generally that this is not the time for entering upon the discussion of amendments: our only question therefore is, how to get rid of the subject.

Representative Roger Sherman of Connecticut, framer of the Constitution and signer of the Declaration of Independence, in the First Congress, June 1789.

VII

THE
BILL
OF
RIGHTS

By this time you have discovered that it is only possible to understand a document like the Constitution in reference to some particular situation—its origins, the personalities of its founders or other conditions. As you read the Bill of Rights you should naturally begin to wonder how it can be explained, at least in part, by the events which preceded its writing. You might look, not only at the events studied in this unit, but at the whole experience of English and American history, and especially at the last years before the American Revolution.

The
Bill
of
Rights

[1791]

ARTICLE THE FIRST. Congress shall make no law respecting the establishment of religion, or prohibiting the free exercise thereof; or abridging the freedom of speech, or of the press; or the right of the people peaceably to assemble, and to petition the government for a redress of grievances.

ARTICLE THE SECOND. A well-regulated militia being necessary to the security of a free State, the right of the people to keep and bears arms shall not be infringed.

ARTICLE THE THIRD. No soldier shall, in time of peace, be quartered in any house without the consent of the owner, nor in time of war, but in a manner prescribed by law.

ARTICLE THE FOURTH. The right of the people to be secure in their persons, houses, papers, and effects, against unreasonable searches and seizures, shall not be violated, and no warrants shall issue, but upon probable cause, supported by oath or affirmation, and particularly describing the place to be searched, and the persons or things to be seized.

ARTICLE THE FIFTH. No person shall be held to answer for a

capital, or otherwise infamous crime, unless on a presentment or indictment of a grand jury, except in cases arising in the land or naval forces, or in the militia, when in actual service in time of war or public danger; nor shall any person be subject for the same offence to be twice put in jeopardy of life or limb; nor shall be compelled in any criminal case to be a witness against himself, nor be deprived of life, liberty, or property, without due process of law; nor shall private property be taken for public use without just compensation.

ARTICLE THE SIXTH. In all criminal prosecutions, the accused shall enjoy the right to a speedy and public trial, by an impartial jury of the State and district wherein the crime shall have been committed, which district shall have been previously ascertained by law, and to be informed of the nature and cause of the accusation; to be confronted with the witnesses against him; to have compulsory process for obtaining witnesses in his favor, and to have the assistance of counsel for his defence.

ARTICLE THE SEVENTH. In suits at common law, where the value in controversy shall exceed twenty dollars, the right of trial by jury shall be preserved, and no fact tried by a jury, shall be otherwise re-examined in any court of the United States than according to the rules of the common law.

ARTICLE THE EIGHTH. Excessive bail shall not be required, nor excessive fines imposed, nor cruel and unusual punishments inflicted.

ARTICLE THE NINTH. The enumeration in the Constitution of certain rights, shall not be construed to deny or disparage others retained by the people.

ARTICLE THE TENTH. The powers not delegated to the United States by the Constitution, nor prohibited by it to the States, are reserved to the States respectively, or to the people.

Congress approved the first ten amendments in their final form for submission to the States in accordance with Article V of the Constitution on August 24, 1789. They were ratified by the required number of states and on December 15, 1791 became a part of the Constitution of the United States. (Massachusetts, incidentally, one of the States to propose amendments, did not ratify the Bill of Rights until 1937 when it did so as part of the ceremonies celebrating the sesquicentennial of the Constitution.)

A. (as a result of the amendments) the great bulk of the late opponents (to the Constitution) are entirely at rest.

Madison to Washington, 1789.

In 1789 North Carolina called its second ratifying convention. The first had voted not to act, a decision that was tantamount to rejection.

B. I think there is no doubt that the North Carolina Convention will adopt the Constitution—the amendments will do the business.

Letter to a North Carolina newspaper, 1789.

C. Mr. Henry appears to me by no means content. But if the people continue as much satisfied, as they at present appear to be, he will be alone in his sentiments.

Letter to Washington, 1789.

D. The opposition to our new Constitution has almost totally disappeared. (A few) indeed have gone to such lengths in their declaration of hostility that they feel awkward perhaps to come over; but the amendments proposed by Congress have brought over almost all their followers . . .

Jefferson to Lafayette, April 1790.

VIII

COMMENTARY

The Constitution has been a continuing source of commentary for historians and scholars, both American and foreign. All the readings which follow—except A—are based on studies of the same material or material similar to what you have been reading. All these sections are history or comments upon history (and sometimes the distinction is hard to make). Still, they represent the kind of statement you might make. If you find no agreement you should not be surprised. After all, as you have probably discovered by now, history does not simply exist, it is written by men. Historians do not merely "discover," they create. The bulk of this section is, of course, devoted to works written since the Constitution was written but the first piece was written by John Adams shortly before the Philadelphia convention. It is obviously, not a direct commentary upon the document. It was primarily a commentary on the constitutions of the states and contained Adams' ideas about constitutions in general. It was, furthermore, an influence on the framers, and it is relevant in reading the excerpts which follow.

A. By the authorities and examples already recited you will be convinced that three branches of power have an unalterable foundation in nature; that they exist in every society natural and artificial; and that, if all of them are not acknowledged in any constitution of government, it will be found to be imperfect, unstable, and soon enslaved; that the legislative and executive authorities are naturally distinct; and that liberty and the laws depend entirely on a separation of them in the frame of government; that the legislative power is naturally and necessarily sovereign and supreme over the executive; and, therefore, that the latter must be made an essential branch of the former, even with a negative, or it will not be able to defend itself, but will be soon invaded, undermined, attacked, or in some way or other totally ruined and annihilated by the former. This is applicable to every state in America in its individual capacity; but is it equally applicable to the United States in their federal capacity?

The people of America and their delegates in congress were of the opinion that a single assembly was every way adequate to the management of all their federal concerns, and with very good reason, because congress is not a legislative assembly. A single council has been found to answer the purposes of confederacies very well. But in all such cases the deputies are responsible to the states, their authority is clearly ascertained, and the states in their separate capacities are the checks. These are able to form an effectual balance and at all times to control their delegates. The security against the dangers of this kind of government will depend upon the accuracy and decision with which the governments of the separate states have their own orders arranged and balanced. The necessity we are under of submitting to a federal government is an additional and a very powerful argument for three branches and a balance by an equal negative in all the separate governments. Congress will always be composed of members from the natural and artificial aristocratical body of every state, even in the northern, as well as in the middle and southern states. Their natural dispositions, then, in general will be (whether they shall be sensible of it or not, and whatever integrity or abilities they may be possessed of) to diminish the prerogatives of the governors and the privileges of the people and to augment the influence of the aristocratical parties. There have been causes enough to prevent the appearance of this inclination hitherto; but a calm course of prosperity would very soon bring it forth, if effectual provision against it be not made in season. It will be found absolutely necessary, therefore, to give negatives to the governors to defend the executive against the influence of this body, as well as the senate and representatives in their several states. The necessity of a negative in the house of representatives will be called in question by nobody . . .

In the present state of society and manners in America, with a people living chiefly by agriculture, in small numbers, sprinkled over large tracts of land, they are not subject to those panics and transports, those contagions of madness and folly, which are seen in countries where large numbers live in small places in daily fear of perishing for want. We know, therefore, that the people can live and increase under almost any kind of government, or without any government at all. But it is of great importance to begin well; misarrangements now made will have great, extensive, and distant consequences; and we are now employed, how little soever we may think of it, in making establishments which will affect the happiness of a hundred millions of inhabitants at a time in a period not very far distant. All nations, under all governments, must have parties; the great secret is to control them. There are but two ways, either by a monarchy and standing army or by a balance in the constitution. Where the people have a voice and there is no balance, there will be everlasting fluctuations, revolutions, and horrors, until a standing army with a general at its head commands the peace, or the necessity of an equilibrium is made apparent to all and is adopted by all.

John Adams, *A Defence of the Constitutions of Government of the United States of America*, 1787.

Among commentators of the nineteenth and twentieth centuries, the ones represented below are generally thought to rank with the most important. The passages which follow are either summaries or excerpts.

The nineteenth century American historian George Bancroft considered the Constitution as a providential gift, a view that reflected much of American thinking of his time. Indeed, even such men as Madison and Franklin sometimes thought of the ratification of the Constitution as so improbable and so vital that only the intervention of Providence could explain it.

Another nineteenth century historian, John Fiske, believed the Constitution was the necessary consequence of the "critical period" (1783–7) and that only a document as inspired and far reaching as the one produced could have saved American society from political and economic disintegration.

The first major historian of the present century was J. Allen Smith.

B.* The popular notion that this Convention in framing the Constitution was actuated solely by a desire to impart more vigor and efficiency to the general government is but a part of the truth. The Convention desired to establish not only a strong and vigorous central government, but one which would at the same time

* J. Allen Smith, *The Spirit of American Government* (1907). Used by permission of the Macmillan Company.

possess great stability or freedom from change . . . This desired stability the government under the Confederation did not possess, since it was, in the opinion of the members of the Convention, dangerously responsive to public opinion; hence their desire to supplant it with an elaborate system of constitutional checks. The triumph of this system was the triumph of a skillfully directed reactionary movement . . .

. . . The preamble began with "We the people," but it was the almost unanimous sentiment of the Convention that the less the people had to do with the government the better. Hamilton wanted to give the rich and well born a "distinct, permanent share in the government." Madison thought the government ought "to protect the minority of the opulent against the majority." . . . From all the evidence . . . the conclusion is irresistible that they sought to establish a form of government which would effectually curb and restrain democracy . . .

Charles Beard became perhaps the most important twentieth century influence in the study of the ratification period.

C.* A majority of the members (of the Convention) were lawyers by profession . . .

Not one member represented in his immediate personal economic interests the small farming or mechanic classes. The overwhelming majority of members, at least five sixths, were immediately, directly, and personally interested in the outcome of their labors at Philadelphia, and were to a greater or less extent economic beneficiaries from the adoption of the Constitution.

* Charles A. Beard, *An Economic Interpretation of the Constitution* (1913). Used by permission of the Macmillan Company.

. . . It is interesting to note that, with the exception of New York, and possibly Delaware, each state had one or more prominent representative in the Convention who held more than a negligible amount of securities, and who could therefore speak with feeling and authority on the question of providing in the new Constitution for the full discharge of the public debt . . .

Washington, of Virginia, was probably the richest man in the United States in his time, and his financial ability was not surpassed among his countrymen anywhere. He possessed, in addition to his great estate on the Potomac, a large amount of fluid capital which he judiciously invested in Western lands . . . he possessed in Virginia . . . more than 35,000 acres valued at $200,000; in Maryland, 1119 acres at $9828 . . . making a grand total of $530,000 . . .

If anyone in the country had a just reason for being disgusted with the imbecilities of the Confederation it was Washington . . .

. . . In all the proceedings of the Convention (Gouverneur) Morris took a deep interest and expressed his views freely, always showing his thorough distrust of democratic institutions . . .

. . . Robert Morris, the merchant prince and speculator of Pennsylvania . . .

. . . Roger Sherman believed in reducing the popular influence in the new government to the minimum . . .

(Beard argued here that most members of the Convention owned national securities or other property—real estate, slaves, etc., whose value would appreciate with the formation of a stronger central government. His contention was that the framers were not idealistic visionaries but hard headed businessmen interested in protecting their property. It was because of this, he said, that the Constitution was a success.)

D. . . . The (Continental) Congress proved a miserable failure. The public debt grew large. Foreign countries refused additional loans. Commerce among the colonies was impossible. The American soldiers were ill-clothed and starving. Rumblings of dissatisfaction arose from every public discussion, and the colonies were on the brink of anarchy.

With such conditions prevailing, amid demands for a strong state government from some, for a strong central government from others, it was a brave group of men indeed who assembled in that Philadelphia convention hall. There was General Washington, the most loved man in the colonies and chairman of the convention; Benjamin Franklin, the colonial wise-acre, grown old in public service; Alexander Hamilton, with his keen logic and youthful fire; James Wilson, Edmund Randolph, James Madison and others . . . With them also was the spirit of all the liberty loving peoples before them. The Bill of Rights, the Magna Charta, the dreams of Rousseau, the cynicism of Voltaire and the practical statement of political principles by Montesquieu, became their guiding influences . . .

Max N. Kroloff, "The Constitution."

E.* That they realized the disastrous economic conditions, that they feared the effect of prevailing unwise and unjust State legislation, and that they expected that a more adequate form of gov-

* Charles Warren, *The Making of the Constitution*, 1929. Boston: Little Brown & Co., p. 54. Reprinted by permission of Mrs. Charles Warren.

ernment would bring an increase of economic prosperity for all classes in the community cannot be doubted. But it is equally indubitable that their leading motive in desiring a new Constitution was their conviction that, without it, a dissolution of the Union and disappearance of republican government were inevitable.

F.* (The Fathers) thought man was a creature of rapacious self-interest, and yet they wanted him to be free—free, in essence, to contend, to engage in an umpired strife, to use property to get property. They accepted the mercantile image of life as an eternal battleground . . . they did not propose to put an end to this war, but merely to stabilize it and make it less murderous. They had no hope and they offered none for any ultimate organic change in the way men conduct themselves. The result was that while they thought self-interest the most dangerous and unbrookable quality of man, they necessarily underwrote it in trying to control it.

Merrill Jensen, a historian of the University of Wisconsin, has conducted one of the most thorough studies of the "Critical Period." He concludes:

G** At the end of the war Americans faced innumerable problems arising from it. What should be done with war veterans?

* Richard Hofstadter, *The American Political Tradition* (1948). Copyright by Alfred A. Knopf, Inc. Used by permission of Alfred A. Knopf, Inc.

** Merrill Jensen, *The New Nation*, 1950. Copyright by Alfred A. Knopf, Inc. and used by permission of Alfred A. Knopf, Inc.

Should the Loyalists return to their homes? What should be our relations with foreign friends and foes? Should commerce be free or should there be discrimination, and if so, against whom and for whose benefit? How would peace affect the economy? How should the war debt be paid? What kind of taxes should be levied to pay it, and who should pay them? When the war-boom collapsed, why did it? Should government encourage one form of economic enterprise over another or should it keep hands off? What about discontented groups: should government ignore them, cater to them, or forcibly suppress those who might revolt?

Such questions or others like them have probably been asked after every great war in history. They were asked, debated, and given various solutions during the 1780's. The significance of those debates and solutions has often been misunderstood. This is no better illustrated than in the case of the national debt during the 1780's which is usually discussed only in terms of depreciation and nonpayment of interest. Actually much more was involved than this. The debt was fantastically low compared with the national debt of today—about twelve dollars per capita as compared with seventeen hundred—and the nation had vast untouched natural resources with which to pay it. Multitudes of accounts had to be reduced to simple forms so that they could be paid, and this the Confederation government managed to do. But even more important than the economics of the national debt was its politics: should it be paid by the states or the central government? A fundamental assumption of every political leader was that the political agency which paid the debt would hold the balance of power in the new nation. Hence, the supporters of a strong central government insisted that the national debt must be paid by Congress while their opponents insisted that it should be divided among the states and paid by them. The latter group was on the way to victory by the end of the 1780's, for they were supported by clamoring creditors. The result was that one state after another assumed portions of the national debt owing to its citizens. Thus the traditional story is so out of context as to be virtually meaningless. This is true of other traditions as well. Most of the ports of the world were open, not closed, to American citizens. Reciprocity and equal treatment of all United States citizens was the rule in the tonnage and tariff acts of the states, not trade barriers.

To say that many of the pessimistic traditions are false is not to say that all Americans were peaceful and satisfied. The holders of national and state debts wanted bigger payments than they got. The merchants wanted more government aid than was given them. The farmers, hit by high taxes and rigid collection of both taxes and private debts, demanded relief in the form of lower taxes and government loans from state legislatures. Such demands kept state politics in an uproar during the 1780's. However, the often violent expression of such discontents in politics should not blind us to the fact that the period was one of extraordinary economic growth. Merchants owned more ships at the end of the 1780's than they had at the beginning of the Revolution, and they carried a greater share of American produce. By 1790 the export of agricultural produce was double what it had been before the war. American cities grew rapidly, with the result that housing was scarce and building booms produced a labor shortage. Tens of thousands of farmers spread outwards to the frontiers. There can be no question but that freedom from the British Empire resulted in a surge of activity in all phases of American life. Of course not all the problems of the new nation were solved by 1789—all have not yet been solved—but there is no evidence of stagnation and decay in the 1780's. Instead the story is one of a newly free people who seized upon every means to improve and enrich themselves in a nation which they believed had a golden destiny.

H.* But why has (the Constitution) survived so long? Why did it not go the way, for example, of the Restoration Charter in France? Has this not been precisely because fundamental value struggles have not been characteristic of the United States? Surely the Constitution did not fare well in the only time any such struggles did appear in the United States, the time of the slavery controversy in the middle of the nineteenth century. Civil war broke out . . . . Would the American Constitution have been able to survive in any nation save one characterized by so much of the "mutual dependence" (agreement on political principles) that Pinckney found here? For the solution the constitutionalists offered to the frightful conflicts they imagined was a complicated scheme of checks and balances which it is reasonable to argue only a highly united nation could make work at all. Delay and deliberate confusion in government became intolerable in communities where men have decisive social programs that they want to execute . . . . The Founding Fathers devised a scheme to deal with conflict that could only survive in a land of solidarity.

I.** With ratification by Virginia and by New Hampshire (which

* From *The Liberal Tradition in America*, © 1955 by Louis Hartz. Used by permission of Harcourt, Brace & World, Inc., pp. 85–86.

** Edward S. Morgan, *The Birth of the Republic,* copyright 1956 by the University of Chicago. Used by permission of the University of Chicago Press. Pp. 155–157.

came in under the Massachusetts formula while the Virginia convention was in progress), the union was assured of ten members, one more than was needed to put the new government into operation. New York followed almost at once. Alexander Hamilton had arranged for express riders to speed the news northward when Virginia should decide, and his messenger arrived in Poughkeepsie, where the New York convention was sitting, in time to frighten a hostile majority of anti-Federalists into adoption (with a long list of interpretations and proposed amendments) lest New York be left in isolation.

Only North Carolina and Rhode Island remained, but the Philadelphia convention had anticipated that some states might balk. That Rhode Island should be one of the recalcitrants served to confirm the somewhat slanderous phrases which had been uttered about her at Philadelphia and subsequently in most of the ratifying conventions. It took North Carolina until November, 1789, and Rhode Island until May, 1790, to join the rest of the United States under the usual formula of recommended amendments.

In spite of the bitter fights that preceded ratification, the differences between Federalists and anti-Federalists were primarily differences of opinion about means, not fundamental differences of principle. Both sides wanted an effective national government. Both sides wanted to guard that government against tyranny. Their disagreement was over the question whether the proposed separation of powers would be an adequate guard. The anti-Federalists thought not, and the amendments they recommended were digested by James Madison (who was also the principal author of the Constitution itself) to become the first ten amendments, usually called the Bill of Rights. These amendments in no way threatened the workability of the new government. Had Madison and his friends had the foresight to include them in the original document, ratification would have been much easier. Instead, it was obtained by the narrowest of margins and by methods that cannot be defended.

The result achieved was so happy that for a century or more those methods were forgotten, and the founding fathers escaped serious criticism. The present century has looked upon the vilification, the pressure, and the politicking, and has sometimes condemned not only the methods but, by implication at least, the result. The Constitution, it has been suggested, represented a reaction from the democratic principles of the Revolution, a reaction engineered by the rich and well-born, which was only overcome by the Jeffersonian and Jacksonian movements that followed.

Everyone who studies the Revolution and the Constitution must decide for himself whether this was true. It is worth pointing out, however, that if the Revolution was a struggle to make property secure, the Constitution was the final fulfillment of that struggle. If the Revolution called for the coupling of taxation with representation, the Constitution made the central government representative before giving it powers to tax. If the Revolution was built upon the principle that all men are created equal, the Constitution gave men a more equal share in the national government than the Confederation did. If the Revolution opened for Americans the discovery of their own nationality, the Constitution gave them the instrument for expressing it. If the Revolution taught them the danger of tyranny, the aim of the Constitution was to prevent tyranny.

Most of us will think it was successful. But the men who made it knew it was not the end of the search. They had come a long way in twenty-five years, perhaps as far as men have ever come in so short a time, but the farther they traveled, the fairer the prospect that lay ahead. The Constitution was a bulwark to protect what they had gained, but it was also a base from which to continue the exploration. The bulwark still stands, and in spite of halts and pauses along the way the exploration still goes on. As long as any man remains less free than another, it cannot honorably cease.

IX

APPENDICES

APPENDIX A

A Brief Chronology

Peace of Paris, ending the Revolution, 1783
Annapolis Convention, 1786
Shays Rebellion, 1786–7
Philadelphia Convention, 1787, spring and summer
Northwest Ordinance Adopted in Congress, 1787
Delaware Ratifies, December 1787
Pennsylvania Ratifies, December 1787
New Jersey Ratifies, December 1787
Georgia Ratifies, January 1788
Connecticut Ratifies, January 1788
Massachusetts Ratifies, February 1788
Maryland Ratifies, April 1788
South Carolina Ratifies, May 1788
Virginia Ratifies, June 1788
New Hampshire Ratifies, June 1788
North Carolina convention fails to ratify, July 1788
New York Ratifies, July 1788
New government forms and Washington is inaugurated, May 1789
Madison asks Congress to consider amendments, June 1789
French Revolution: storming of the Bastille, July 1789
Congress approves amendments, August 1789
North Carolina Ratifies, November 1789
Rhode Island Ratifies, May 1790
Amendments become part of the Constitution, December 1791

APPENDIX B

Madison's *Federalist* #10 presents clearly many of the assumptions which the writers of the Constitution held about the nature of man and about his behavior in society. (See also John Adams's comments in Section VII.) The Constitution has often been called a realistic document; the following number of *The Federalist*—one of the classics of the series—gives some of the reasons why.

The Federalist

To the People of the State of New York:

Among the numerous advantages promised by a well-constructed Union, none deserves to be more accurately developed than its tendency to break and control the violence of faction. The friend of popular governments never finds himself so much alarmed for their character and fate, as when he contemplates their propensity to this dangerous vice. He will not fail, therefore, to set a due value on any plan which, without violating the principles to which he is attached, provides a proper cure for it. The instability, injustice, and confusion introduced into the public councils, have, in truth, been the mortal diseases under which popular governments have everywhere perished; as they continue to be the favorite and fruitful topics from which the adversaries to liberty derive their most specious declamations. The valuable improvements made by the American constitutions on the popular models, both ancient and modern, cannot certainly be too much admired; but it would be an unwarrantable partiality, to contend that they have as effectually obviated the danger on this side, as was wished and expected. Complaints are everywhere heard from our most considerate and virtuous citizens, equally the friends of public and private faith, and of public and personal liberty, that our governments are too unstable, that the public good is disregarded in the conflicts of rival parties, and that measures are too often decided, not according to the rules of justice and the rights of the minor party, but by the superior force of an interested and overbearing majority. However anxiously we may wish that these complaints had no foundation, the evidence of known facts will not permit us to deny that they are in some degree true. It will be found, indeed, on a candid review of our situation, that some of the distresses under which we labor have been erroneously charged on the operation of our governments; but it will be found, at the same time, that other causes will not alone account for many of our heaviest misfortunes; and, particularly, for that prevailing and increasing distrust of public engagements, and alarm for private rights, which are echoed from one end of the continent to the other. These must be chiefly, if not wholly, effects of the unsteadiness and injustice with which a factious spirit has tainted our public administrations.

By a faction, I understand a number of citizens, whether amounting to a majority or minority of the whole, who are united and actuated by some common impulse of passion, or of interest, adverse to the rights of other citizens, or to the permanent and aggregate interests of the community. There are two methods of curing the mischiefs of faction; the one, by removing its causes; the other, by controlling its effects.

There are again two methods of removing the causes of faction: the one, by destroying the liberty which is essential to its existence; the other, by giving to every citizen the same opinions, the same passions, the same interests.

It could never be more truly said than of the first remedy, that it was worse than the disease. Liberty is to faction what air is to fire, an ailment without which it instantly expires. But it could not be less folly to abolish liberty, which is essential to political life, because it nourishes faction, than it would do to wish the annihilation of air, which is essential to animal life, because it imparts to fire its destructive agency.

The second expedient is as impracticable as the first would be unwise. As long as the reason of man continues fallible, and he is at liberty to exercise it, different opinions will be formed. As long as the connection subsists between his reason and his self-love, his opinions and his passions will have a reciprocal influence on each other; and the former will be objects to which the latter will attach themselves.

The diversity in the faculties of men, from which the rights of property originate, is not less an insuperable obstacle to a uniformity of interests. The protection of these faculties is the first object of government. From the protection of different and unequal faculties of acquiring property, the possession of different degrees and kinds of property immediately results; and from the influence of these on the sentiments and views of the respective proprietors, ensues a division of the society into different interests and parties.

The latent causes of faction are thus sown in the nature of man; and we see them everywhere brought into different degrees of activity, according to the different circumstances of civil society. A zeal for different opinions concerning religion, concerning government, and many other points, as well of speculation as of practice; an attachment of different leaders ambitiously contending for pre-eminence and power; or to persons of other descriptions whose fortunes have been interesting to the human passions, have, in turn, divided mankind into parties, inflamed them with mutual animosity, and rendered them much more disposed to vex and oppress each other than to co-operate for their common good. So strong is this propensity of mankind to fall into mutual animosities, that where no substantial occasion presents itself, the most frivolous and fanciful distinctions have been sufficient to kindle their unfriendly passions and excite their most violent conflicts. But the most common and durable source of factions has been the various and unequal distribution of property. Those who hold and those who are without property have ever formed distinct interests in society. Those who are creditors, and those who are debtors, fall under a like discrimination. A landed interest, a manufacturing interest, a mercantile interest, a moneyed interest, with many lesser interests, grow up of necessity in civilized nations, and divide them into different classes, actuated by different sentiments and views. The regulation of these various and interfering interests forms the principal task of modern legislation, and involves the spirit of party and faction in the necessary and ordinary operations of the government.

No man is allowed to be a judge in his own cause, because his interest would certainly bias his judgment, and, not improbably, corrupt his integrity. With equal, nay with greater reason, a body of men are unfit to be both judges and parties at the same time; yet what are many of the most important acts of legislation, but so many judicial determinations, not indeed concerning the rights of single persons, but concerning the rights of large bodies of citizens? And what are the different classes of legislators but advocates and parties to the causes which they determine? Is a law proposed concerning private debts? It is a question to which the creditors are parties on one side and the debtors on the other. Justice ought to hold the balance between them. Yet the parties are, and must be, themselves the judges; and the most numerous party, or, in other words, the most powerful faction must be expected to prevail. Shall domestic manufactures be encouraged, and in what degree, by restrictions on foreign manufactures? are questions which would be differently decided by the landed and the manufacturing classes, and probably by neither with a sole regard to justice and the public good. The apportionment of taxes on the various descriptions of property is an act which seems to require the most exact impartiality; yet there is, perhaps, no legislative act in which greater opportunity and temptation are given to a predominant party to trample on the rules of justice. Every shilling with which they overburden the inferior number, is a shilling saved to their own pockets.

It is in vain to say that enlightened statesmen will be able to adjust these clashing interests, and render them all subservient to the public good. Enlightened statesmen will not always be at the helm. Nor, in many cases, can such an adjustment be made at all without taking into view indirect and remote considerations, which will rarely prevail over the immediate interests which one party may find in disregarding the rights of another or the good of the whole.

The inference to which we are brought is, that the *causes* of faction cannot be removed, and that relief is only to be sought in the means of controlling its *effects*.

If a faction consists of less than a majority, relief is supplied by the republican principle, which enables the majority to defeat its sinister views by regular vote. It may clog the administration, it may convulse the society; but it will be unable to execute and mask its violence under the forms of the Constitution. When a majority is included in a faction, the form of popular government, on the other hand, enables it to sacrifice to its ruling passion or interest both the public good and the rights of other citizens. To secure the public good and private rights against the danger of such a faction, and at the same time to preserve the spirit and the form of popular government, is then the great object to which our inquiries are directed. Let me add that it is the great desideratum by which this form of government can be rescued from the approbrium under which it has so long labored, and be recommended to the esteem and adoption of mankind.

By what means is this object attainable? Evidently by one of two only. Either the existence of the same passion or interest in a majority at the same time must be prevented, or the majority, having such coexistent passion or interest, must be rendered, by their number and local situation, unable to concert and carry into effect schemes of oppression. If the impulse and the opportunity be suffered to coincide, we well know that neither moral nor religious motives can be relied on as an adequate control. They are not found to be such on the injustice and violence of individuals, and lose their efficacy in proportion to the number combined together, that is, in proportion as their efficacy becomes needful.

From this view of the subject it may be concluded that a pure democracy, by which I mean a society consisting of a small number of citizens, who assemble and administer the government in person, can admit of no cure for the mischiefs of faction. A common passion or interest will, in almost every case, be felt by a majority of the whole; a communication and concert result from the form of government itself; and there is nothing to check the inducements to sacrifice the weaker party or an obnoxious individual. Hence it is that such democracies have ever been spectacles of turbulence and contention; have ever been found incompatible with personal security or the rights of property; and have in general been as short in their lives as they have been violent in their deaths. Theoretic politicians, who have patronized this species of government, have erroneously supposed that by reducing mankind to a perfect equality in their political rights, they would, at the same time, be perfectly equalized and assimilated in their possessions, their opinions, and their passions.

A republic, by which I mean a government in which the scheme of representation takes place, opens a different prospect, and promises the cure for which we are seeking. Let us examine the points in which it varies from pure democracy and we shall comprehend both the nature of the cure and the efficacy which it must derive from the Union.

The two great points of difference between a democracy and a republic are: first, the delegation of the government, in the latter, to a small number of citizens elected by the rest; secondly, the greater number of citizens, and greater sphere of country, over which the latter may be extended. The effect of the first difference is, on the one hand, to refine and enlarge the public views, by passing them through the medium of a chosen body of citizens, whose wisdom may best discern the true interest of their country, and whose patriotism and love of justice will be least likely to sacrifice it to temporary or partial considerations. Under such a regulation, it may well happen that the public voice, pronounced by the representatives of the people, will be more consonant to the public good than if pronounced by the people themselves, convened for the purpose. On the other hand, the effect may be inverted. Men of factious tempers, of local prejudices, or of sinister designs, may, by intrigue, by corruption, or by other means, first obtain the suffrages, and then betray the interests, of the people. The question resulting is, whether small or extensive republics are more favorable to the election of proper guardians of the public weal; and it is clearly decided in favor of the latter by two obvious considerations: In the first place, it is to be remarked that, however small the republic may be, the representatives must be raised to a certain number, in order to guard against the cabals of a few; and that, however large it may be, they must be limited to a certain number, in order to guard against the confusion of a multitude. Hence, the number of representatives in the two cases not being in proportion to that of the two constituents, and being proportionally greater in the small republic, it follows that, if the proportion of fit characters be not less in the large than in the small republic, the former will present a greater option, and consequently a greater probability of a fit choice.

In the next place, as each representative will be chosen by a greater number of citizens in the large than in the small republic, it will be more difficult for unworthy candidates to practise with success the vicious arts by which elections are too often carried; and the suffrages of the people being more free, will be more likely to centre in men who possess the most attractive merit and the most diffusive and established characters.

It must be confessed that in this, as in most other cases, there is a mean, on both sides of which inconveniences will be found to lie. By enlarging too much the number of electors, you render the representative too little acquainted with all their local circumstances and lesser interests; as by reducing it too much, you render him unduly attached to these, and too little fit to comprehend and pursue great and national objects. The federal Constitution forms a happy combination in this respect; the great and aggregate interests being referred to the national, the local and particular to the State legislatures.

The other point of difference is, the greater number of citizens and extent of territory which may be brought within the compass

of republican than of democratic government; and it is this circumstance principally which renders factious combinations less
to be dreaded in the former than in the latter. The smaller the
society, the fewer probably will be the distinct parties and interests composing it; the fewer the distinct parties and interests, the
more frequently will a majority be found of the same party; and
the smaller the number of individuals composing a majority, and
the smaller the compass within which they are placed, the more
easily will they concert and execute their plans of oppression.
Extend the sphere and you take in a greater variety of parties and
interests; you make it less probable that a majority of the whole
will have a common motive to invade the rights of other citizens;
or if such a common motive exists, it will be more difficult for all
who feel it to discover their own strength, and to act in unison
with each other. Besides other impediments, it may be remarked
that, where there is a consciousness of unjust or dishonorable purposes, communication is always checked by distrust in proportion
to the number whose concurrence is necessary.

Hence, it clearly appears, that the same advantage which a
republic has over a democracy, in controlling the effects of faction, is enjoyed by a large over a small republic,—is enjoyed by
the Union over the States composing it. Does the advantage consist in the substitution of representatives whose enlightened views
and virtuous sentiments render them superior to local prejudices
and to schemes of injustice? It will not be denied that the representation of the Union will be most likely to possess these requisite endowments. Does it consist in the greater security afforded
by a greater variety of parties, against the event of any one party
being able to outnumber and oppress the rest? In an equal degree
does the increased variety of parties comprised within the Union,
increase this security. Does it, in fine, consist in the greater

obstacles opposed to the concert and accomplishment of the secret wishes of an unjust and interested majority? Here, again, the extent of the Union gives it the most palpable advantage.

The influence of factious leaders may kindle a flame within their particular States, but will be unable to spread a general conflagration through the other States. A religious sect may degenerate into a political faction in a part of the Confederacy; but the variety of sects dispersed over the entire face of it must secure the national councils against any danger from that source. A rage for paper money, for an abolition of debts, for an equal division of property, or for any other improper or wicked project, will be less apt to pervade the whole body of the Union than a particular member of it; in the same proportion as such a malady is more likely to taint a particular county or district, than an entire state.

In the extent and proper structure of the Union, therefore, we behold a republican remedy for the diseases most incident to republican government. And according to the degree of pleasure and pride we feel in being republicans, ought to be our zeal in cherishing the spirit and supporting the character of Federalists.

—PUBLIUS

Madison, in *The Federalist* #10, 1787.

APPENDIX C

Some Remarks About Bibliography

Some of the readings in this manual are difficult, and it is likely that there will be some passages which you do not understand or references for which you are not prepared. If you do not understand the gist of a section try to read over the parts which puzzle you, or ask your teacher.

You will discover, as you work in this unit, that there is little agreement about many things in the period you are studying. This is not exceptional in history or in most other disciplines. This disagreement is reflected in the readings and in the bibliography.

Generally historians divide their bibliographies under the headings "original sources" and "secondary sources." Sometimes this distinction is hard to make. Nevertheless, original sources (and this manual is almost entirely composed of such material) are generally letters, documents, newspaper accounts, economic statistics, or other material produced at close hand to the subject under study. Secondary sources, in contrast, are conclusions and generalizations drawn from these sources. Thus, an entry in a county clerk's office recording the birth of Lincoln would be an original source. A statement in a history book published last year, stating that Lincoln was born at a certain time in a certain place, is a secondary source. Letters from soldiers and officers of the civil war, battle orders, etc., are original sources. A chapter in a book by the modern historian Bruce Catton is a secondary source. Secondary sources are usually conclusions and generalizations based directly or indirectly on original sources.

The following works are most important as original sources on the Constitution: Max Farrand, *The Records of the Federal Convention,*

New Haven, 1911; Jonathan Elliott, *The Debates in the Several State Conventions on the Adoption of the Federal Constitution* (5 vols.), Philadelphia, 1859; *Documentary History of the Constitution of the United States of America* (5 vols.), Washington, 1905; *The Annals of Congress.* In addition there are collections of the writings of Washington, Hamilton, Madison, Jay, James Wilson, Rufus King, Benjamin Franklin and many others. Much of the material in this manual comes from these works. There are also separate accounts of the State conventions of many states, among them F. G. Bates, *Rhode Island and the Formation of the Union,* and John B. McMaster and Fred Stone, *Pennsylvania and the Federal Constitution.*

Additional comments and debates about the Constitution are, of course, included in *The Federalist,* by Hamilton, Jay and Madison, which has appeared in various editions, including the Modern Library. Excerpts are also available in a very inexpensive paperback edition; Paul L. Ford's *Pamphlets on the Constitution* includes newspaper essays of the time, including Richard Henry Lee's "Letters from a Farmer." In addition of course, there is much material in the newspapers of the time, in various orations, and in sermons delivered from the pulpit. A careful historian might even look at newspaper advertisements to acquire some notion of the economy of the age. You must not forget, however, that the most important single source is the Constitution itself.

Secondary sources are even more varied. Nearly all of the material in Section VIII of this booklet is drawn from secondary sources. Your textbook is a secondary source of a kind. *The Framing of the Constitution,* by Max Farrand, 1913, is a good account of the Philadelphia convention as is Carl Van Doren's *The Great Rehearsal,* 1948. Charles Beard has had many followers as well as critics. Among the followers is Fred Roddell whose *Fifty-five Men* is a wholesale attack on the framers. Beard has also had severe critics since 1913 when his *Economic Interpretation of the Constitution* was published and when

Theodore Roosevelt accused him of "muckraking the Constitution" to the present day. In 1956 Robert E. Brown dissected his arguments in *Charles Beard and the Constitution* and just recently, Forrest Mac-Donald, another historian, issued what amounted to a dollar for dollar argument against Beard in a book called *We the People*.

To understand the Constitution more fully it will be helpful not only to read contemporary accounts and subsequent commentary, but also to study the events and ideas which preceded its formulation (this goes, of course, for the study of any historical event). Throughout the debates, the writers of the Constitution quoted and referred to thinkers like Montesquieu and Locke, to the events of the pre-Revolutionary years in America, to the experiences of the Swiss, the Dutch, the English and many other nations in organizing government.

Biographies of the figures who took part in the events in which you are interested are always useful; indeed they often shed clues which would be hard to find otherwise. For all men, even the great, are motivated by a variety of considerations; sometimes they are selfish, sometimes they are superstitious; they do not always act rationally, they lose their tempers; sometimes they contradict themselves, sometimes they say one thing and do another.

In writing accounts of events long past historians are frequently motivated by the events of their own time. Charles Beard produced his *Economic Interpretation* at a time when many American institutions, including the Supreme Court and the Constitution were the subjects of bitter controversy, the controversy arising from the Progressive Era's challenge against the dominant political and economic forces of its time; foreign wars often generate historical writing that is more nationalistic than work produced in peacetime, reflecting the temper of the age which produced it. A history of ratification written today may become an *original source* for a historian who, at some future time, undertakes a study of the events and attitudes of the 1960's.

APPENDIX D

Amendments 11–23

ARTICLE THE ELEVENTH. The judicial power of the United States shall not be construed to extend to any suit in law or equity, commenced or prosecuted against one of the United States by citizens of another State, or by citizens or subjects of any foreign State.

ARTICLE THE TWELFTH. The electors shall meet in their respective States and vote by ballot for President and Vice-President, one of whom, at least, shall not be an inhabitant of the same State with themselves; they shall name in their ballots the person voted for as President, and in distinct ballots the person voted for as Vice-President, and they shall make distinct lists of all persons voted for as President and of all persons voted for as Vice-President, and of the number of votes for each; which lists they shall sign and certify, and transmit sealed to the seat of the government of the United States, directed to the President of the Senate. The President of the Senate shall, in the presence of the Senate and House of Representatives, open all the certificates and the votes shall then be counted. The person having the greatest number of votes for President shall be the President, if such number be a majority of the whole number of Electors appointed; and if no person have such majority, then from the persons having the highest numbers not exceeding three on the list of those voted for as President, the House of Representatives shall choose immediately, by ballot, the President. But in choosing the President the votes shall be taken by States, the representation from each State having one vote; a quorum for this purpose shall consist of a member or members from two-thirds of the States, and a majority of all the States shall be necessary to a choice. And if the House of Representatives shall not choose a President whenever the right of choice shall devolve upon them, before the fourth day of March next following, then the Vice-President shall act as President as in the case of the death or other constitutional disability of the President.

The person having the greatest number of votes as Vice-President shall be the Vice-President, if such number be a majority of the whole number of Electors appointed; and if no person have a majority, then from the two highest numbers on the list the Senate shall choose the Vice-President; a quorum for the purpose shall consist of two-thirds of the whole number of Senators, and a majority of the whole number shall be necessary to a choice.

But no person constitutionally ineligible to the office of President shall be eligible to that of Vice-President of the United States.

ARTICLE THE THIRTEENTH. SECTION 1. Neither slavery nor involuntary servitude, except as a punishment for crime whereof the party shall have been duly convicted, shall exist within the United States, or any place subject to their jurisdiction.

SECTION 2. Congress shall have power to enforce this article by appropriate legislation.

ARTICLE THE FOURTEENTH. SECTION 1. All persons born or naturalized in the United States, and subject to the jurisdiction thereof, are citizens of the United States and of the State wherein they reside. No State shall make or enforce any law which shall abridge the privileges or immunities of citizens of the United States; nor shall any State deprive any person of life, liberty or property without due process of law; nor deny to any person within its jurisdiction the equal protection of the laws.

SECTION 2. Representatives shall be apportioned among the several States according to their respective numbers, counting the whole number of persons in each State, excluding Indians not taxed. But when the right to vote at any election for the choice of Electors for President and Vice-President of the United States, representatives in Congress, the executive and judicial officers of a State, or the members of the legislature thereof, is denied to any of the male inhabitants of such State, being twenty-one years of age, and citizens of the United States, or in any way abridged except for participation in rebellion or other crime, the basis of representation therein shall be reduced in the proportion which the number of such male citizens shall bear to the whole number of male citizens twenty-one years of age in such State.

SECTION 3. No person shall be a senator or representative in Congress, or elector of President and Vice-President, or hold any office, civil or military, under the United States or under any State, who, having previously taken an oath as a member of Congress, or as an officer of the United States, or as a member of any State legislature, or as an executive or judicial officer of any State, to support the Constitution of the United States, shall have engaged in insurrection or rebellion against the same, or given aid or comfort to the enemies thereof. But Congress may, by a vote of two-thirds of each House, remove such disability.

SECTION 4. The validity of the public debt of the United States, authorized by law, including debts incurred for payment of pensions and bounties for services in suppressing insurrection or rebellion, shall not be questioned. But neither the United States nor any State shall assume or pay any debt or obligation incurred in aid of insurrection or rebellion against the United States, or any claim for the loss or emancipation of any slave; but all such debts, obligations, and claims shall be held illegal and void.

SECTION 5. The Congress shall have power to enforce, by appropriate legislation, the provisions of this article.

ARTICLE THE FIFTEENTH. SECTION 1. The right of citizens of the United States to vote shall not be denied or abridged by the United States, or by any State, on account of race, color, or previous condition of servitude.

SECTION 2. The Congress shall have power to enforce this article by appropriate legislation.

ARTICLE THE SIXTEENTH. The Congress shall have the power to lay and collect taxes on incomes, from whatever source derived, without apportionment among the several States, and without regard to any census or enumeration.

ARTICLE THE SEVENTEENTH. SECTION 1. The Senate of the United States shall be composed of two Senators from each State, elected by the people thereof, for six years; and each Senator shall have one vote. The electors in each State shall have the qualifications requisite for electors of the most numerous branch of the State legislatures.

SECTION 2. When vacancies happen in the representation of any State in the Senate, the executive authority of such State shall issue writs of election to fill such vacancies: Provided, that the legislature of any State may empower the executive thereof to make temporary appointments until the people fill the vacancies by election as the legislature may direct.

SECTION 3. This amendment shall not be so construed as to affect the election or term of any Senator chosen before it becomes valid as part of the Constitution.

ARTICLE THE EIGHTEENTH. SECTION 1. After one year from the ratification* of this article the manufacture, sale or transportation

* Jan. 16, 1919.

of intoxicating liquors within, the importation thereof into, or the exportation thereof from the United States and all territory subject to the jurisdiction thereof, for beverage purposes, is hereby prohibited.

SECTION 2. The Congress and the several States shall have concurrent power to enforce this article by appropriate legislation.

SECTION 3. This article shall be inoperative unless it shall have been ratified as an amendment to the Constitution by the legislatures of the several States, as provided in the Constitution, within seven years from the date of the submission hereof to the States by the Congress.

ARTICLE THE NINETEENTH. SECTION 1. The right of citizens of the United States to vote shall not be denied or abridged by the United States or by any State on account of sex.

SECTION 2. Congress shall have power to enforce this article by appropriate legislation.

ARTICLE THE TWENTIETH. SECTION 1. The terms of the President and Vice-President shall end at noon on the twentieth day of January, and the terms of Senators and Representatives at noon on the third day of January, of the years in which such terms would have ended if this article had not been ratified; and the terms of their successors shall then begin.

SECTION 2. The Congress shall assemble at least once in every year, and such meeting shall begin at noon on the third day of January, unless they shall by law appoint a different day.

SECTION 3. If, at the time fixed for the beginning of the term of the President, the President-elect shall have died, the Vice-President-elect shall become President. If a President shall not have been chosen before the time fixed for the beginning of his term or if the President-elect shall have failed to qualify, then the Vice-President-elect shall act as President until a President shall have qualified; and the Congress may by law provide for the case wherein neither a President-elect nor a Vice-President-elect shall have qualified, declaring who shall then act as President, or the manner in which one who is to act shall be selected, and such persons shall act accordingly until a President or Vice-President shall have qualified.

SECTION 4. The Congress may by law provide for the case of the death of any of the persons from whom the House of Representatives may choose a President whenever the right of choice shall have devolved upon them, and for the case of the death of any of the persons from whom the Senate may choose a Vice-President whenever the right of choice shall have devolved upon them.

SECTION 5. Sections 1 and 2 shall take effect on the fifteenth day of October following the ratification of this article.

SECTION 6. This article shall be inoperative unless it shall have been ratified as an amendment to the Constitution by the legislatures of three-fourths of the several States within seven years from the date of its submission.

ARTICLE THE TWENTY–FIRST. SECTION 1. The eighteenth article of amendment to the Constitution of the United States is hereby repealed.

SECTION 2. This article shall be inoperative unless it shall have been ratified as an amendment to the Constitution by the legislators of three-fourths of the several States within seven years from the date of its submission to the States by the Congress.

SECTION 3. This article shall be inoperative unless it shall have been ratified as an amendment to the Constitution by conventions in the several States, as provided in the Constitution, within seven years from the date of the submission hereof to the States by the Congress.

ARTICLE THE TWENTY–SECOND. SECTION 1. No person shall be elected to the office of the President more than twice. No person who has held the office of the President or acted as President for more than two years of a term to which some other person was elected President shall be elected to the office of the President more than once. But this article shall not apply to any person holding the office of President when this article was proposed by the Congress and shall not prevent any person who may be holding the office of President or acting as President during the term within which this article becomes operative from holding the office of President or acting as President during the remainder of such a term.

SECTION 2. This article shall be inoperative unless it shall have been ratified as an amendment to the Constitution by the legislators of three-fourths of the several States within seven years from the date of its submission to the States by the Congress.

ARTICLE THE TWENTY-THIRD. SECTION 1. The District constituting the seat of Government of the United States shall appoint in such manner as the Congress may direct: A number of electors of President and Vice President equal to the whole number of Senators and Representatives in Congress to which the District would be entitled if it were a State, but in no event more than the least populous State; they shall be in addition to those appointed by the States, but they shall be considered, for the purposes of the election of President and Vice President, to be electors appointed by a State; and they shall meet in the District and perform such duties as provided by the twelfth article of amendment.

SECTION 2. The Congress shall have power to enforce this article by appropriate legislation.

The
Declaration
of
Independence

[1776]

WHEN, in the course of human events, it becomes necessary for one people to dissolve the political bands which have connected them with another, and to assume, among the powers of the earth, the separate and equal station to which the laws of nature and of nature's God entitle them, a decent respect to the opinions of mankind requires that they should declare the causes which impel them to the separation.

We hold these truths to be self-evident, that all men are created equal; that they are endowed by their Creator with certain unalienable rights; that among these, are life, liberty, and the pursuit of happiness. That, to secure these rights, governments are instituted among men, deriving their just powers from the consent of the governed; that, whenever any form of government becomes destructive of these ends, it is the right of the people to alter or to abolish it and to institute new government, laying its foundation on such principles and organizing its powers in such form, as to them shall seem most likely to effect their safety and happiness. Prudence, indeed, will dictate that governments long established should not be changed for light and transient causes; and accordingly all experience hath shown, that mankind are more disposed to suffer, while evils are sufferable, than to right themselves by abolishing the forms to which they are accustomed. But when a long train of abuses and usurpations, pursuing invariably the same object, evinces a design to reduce them under absolute despotism, it is their right, it is their duty, to throw off such government, and to provide new guards for their future security. Such has been the patient sufferance of these colonies; and such is now the necessity which constrains them to alter their former systems of government. The history of the present king of Great Britain is a history of repeated injuries and usurpations, all having in direct object the establishment of an absolute tyranny over these States. To prove this, let facts be submitted to a candid world.

He has refused his assent to laws the most wholesome and necessary for the public good.

He has forbidden his Governors to pass laws of immediate and pressing importance, unless suspended in their operation till his assent should be obtained; and, when so suspended, he has utterly neglected to attend to them.

He has refused to pass other laws for the accommodation of large districts of people, unless those people would relinquish the right of representation in the legislature, a right inestimable to them and formidable to tyrants only.

He has called together legislative bodies at places unusual, uncomfortable, and distant from the depository of their public records, for the sole purpose of fatiguing them into compliance with his measures.

He has dissolved representative houses repeatedly, for opposing with manly firmness his invasions on the rights of the people.

He has refused for a long time, after such dissolutions, to cause others to be elected; whereby the legislative powers, incapable of annihilation, have returned to the people at large for their exercise; the State remaining in the meantime exposed to all the dangers of invasion from without, and convulsions within.

He has endeavored to prevent the population of these States; for that purpose obstructing the laws of naturalization of foreigners; refusing to pass others to encourage their migration hither, and raising the conditions of new appropriations of lands.

He has obstructed the administration of justice, by refusing his assent to laws for establishing judiciary powers.

He has made judges dependent on his will alone, for the tenure of their offices, and the amount and payment of their salaries.

He has erected a multitude of new offices, and sent hither swarms of officers to harass our people, and eat out their substance.

He has kept among us, in times of peace, standing armies without the consent of our legislatures.

He has affected to render the military independent of, and superior to, the civil power.

He has combined with others to subject us to a jurisdiction foreign to our constitution and unacknowledged by our laws; giving his assent to their acts of pretended legislation:

For quartering large bodies of armed troops among us;

For protecting them, by a mock trial, from punishment, for any murders which they should commit on the inhabitants of these States;

For cutting off our trade with all parts of the world;

For imposing taxes on us without our consent;

For depriving us, in many cases, of the benefits of trial by jury;

For transporting us beyond seas to be tried for pretended offences;

For abolishing the free system of English laws in a neighboring province, establishing therein an arbitrary government, and enlarging its boundaries so as to render it at once an example and fit instrument for introducing the same absolute rule into these colonies;

For taking away our charters, abolishing our most valuable laws, and altering fundamentally the forms of our government;

For suspending our own legislatures, and declaring themselves invested with power to legislate for us in all cases whatsoever.

He has abdicated government here, by declaring us out of his protection and waging war against us.

He has plundered our seas, ravaged our coasts, burnt our towns, and destroyed the lives of our people.

He is at this time transporting large armies of foreign mercenaries to complete the works of death, desolation, and tyranny, already begun, with circumstances of cruelty and perfidy scarcely paralleled in the most barbarous ages and totally unworthy the head of a civilized nation.

He has constrained our fellow-citizens, taken captive on the high seas, to bear arms against their country, to become the executioners of their friends and brethren, or to fall themselves by their hands.

He has excited domestic insurrections amongst us, and has endeavored to bring on the inhabitants of our frontiers, the merciless Indian savages, whose known rule of warfare is an undistinguished destruction of all ages, sexes, and conditions.

In every stage of these oppressions we have petitioned for redress, in the most humble terms: Our repeated petitions have been answered only by repeated injury. A prince whose character is thus marked by every act which may define a tyrant is unfit to be the ruler of a free people.

Nor have we been wanting in attention to our British brethren. We have warned them from time to time of attempts by their legislature to extend an unwarrantable jurisdiction over us. We have reminded them of the circumstances of our emigration and settlement here. We have appealed to their native justice and magnanimity, and we have conjured them by the ties of our common kindred to disavow these usurpations which would inevitably interrupt our connections and correspondence. They too have been deaf to the voice of justice and consanguinity. We must, therefore, acquiesce in the necessity which denounces our separation, and hold them, as we hold the rest of mankind, enemies in war, in peace friends.

We, therefore, the Representatives of the United States of America, in General Congress assembled, appealing to the Supreme Judge of the World for the rectitude of our intentions, do, in the name, and by authority of the good people of these colonies, solemnly publish and declare, That these United Colonies are, and of right ought to be, free and independent States; that they are absolved from all allegiance to the British crown, and that all political connection between them and the state of Great Britain, is, and ought to be, totally dissolved; and that, as free and independent states, they have full power to levy war, conclude peace, contract alliances, establish commerce, and to do all other acts and things which independent States may of right do. And for the support of this declaration, with a firm reliance on the protection of Divine Providence, we mutually pledge to each other our lives, our fortunes, and our sacred honor.

[Signatures omitted]

NOTES

NOTES

NOTES

TEACHER'S EDITION

FOR

THE RATIFICATION OF THE CONSTITUTION

AND THE BILL OF RIGHTS

Teacher's Edition

THE RATIFICATION OF THE CONSTITUTION AND
THE BILL OF RIGHTS

The intent of this unit is to put the student in a position where he must work out his own "history" of this topic. In general it is hoped that, except for background, he will not be given any conclusions about the material presented, that he will be led by Socratic questions to form his own statements and, in the process, learn some of the techniques and some of the limitations of the historical approach.

It need not be pointed out that this kind of learning procedure puts the teacher in a position different from that of a lecturer. It may well be a very much more difficult position. Nevertheless, the unit may also prove to be an exciting experience.

The outline which follows is intended more as a definition or an example than as a rigid guide for the teacher. It is impossible to anticipate the most fruitful tacks of discussion for any particular situation.

The scheme of the unit is to take the student from a position of ignorance almost directly to the sources and to lead him to increasingly broad and sophisticated statements about the subject. Repeatedly along the way he should be asked to write short papers, not as a means of testing him but merely as a way of making him think. There is no need for the teacher to do more than sample the papers of the students. The student should understand that the papers are primarily teaching devices and not tests. They are intended to force the student to make statements, to realize the difficulty of this process and to appreciate something of the tentative nature of all history. Clearly the papers should be of some use in planning and stimulating class discussions. Needless to say, one carefully defined sentence in such papers is more valuable than a page of glorious generalizations.

There is no need to point out the corollary advantages and difficulties of such a process. The advantages include, among others, the reading of original sources rather than the memorization of textbook "facts," the employment of inductive reasoning, and the process of frequent, brief writing. The difficulties are obvious. The source materials are not always easy reading and hence have been kept at an absolute minimum. Thought itself is never easy, and writing is often a torture. Furthermore, the difficulties of a sudden introduction of such techniques are bound to be greater than they would be if the techniques were familiar. Nevertheless, the novelty, the change of pace from the routine of the past, may also provide a stimulating balance to some of these difficulties. Given the difficulties, the teacher is freed from the obligation of planning lectures. The unit was designed with the assumption that the teacher's energies would be concentrated in planning and leading discussions and, if possible, working individually with students.

Originally a detailed outline, a kind of lesson plan, had been prepared. But it was felt that this procedure would be too rigid. However, in order to define the procedure that is intended, certain questions and objectives are spelled out as suggestions. The questions can be used as definitions for short papers or for class discussion or, preferably, for both. The questions are not objective—they are merely guides for writing or for the discussion, to help lead the student from one step to the next.

For convenience the unit is divided into eight parts. Part I is for class work on the first day (Monday), the others are for work at home. The last day (Friday of the second week) is saved for an examination. In trials in a number of classes some teachers found the time allowed too short. You may wish to go at a slower pace, especially with slower sections.

The success of the unit hinges on the teacher's ability to make students organize the material that is presented, to articulate conclusions, and to understand the limitations of those conclusions.

There is, of course, nothing terribly logical about history. Its events often seem to be unrelated, paradoxical, or fragmentary. Here, as in all disciplines, logic comes only with the mind of the scholar or the student who tries to organize the events and the ideas. There is nothing intrinsic about history; it does not organize itself; the mind must do that. One man's account of a battle, for instance, is better than another's (closer to the "truth") simply because it seems to provide more reasonable connections between events and between ideas.

It is with these things in mind that this unit was prepared. Its intent is simply to present a limited amount of documentary evidence each day and to ask the student to organize an ever-increasing area of experience. Yet as he does this he should also be aware of the limitations of any such organization, not only because he has only limited access to information, because huge areas are entirely left out, but because any statement in any discipline is tentative and to some extent subjective.

Specifically, of course, he is supposed to learn something of the history of the Constitution, and it is hoped that the techniques suggested will do this far more effectively than teaching from a textbook. Primarily he should learn that the Constitution was the result of a series of demands, that it was made by men, not demigods, who drew on prior experience. He should realize what was "critical" about the "critical period" and what was not. He should learn, furthermore, that the country did not rush to adopt it, but that ratification came only after a number of hard struggles in which honest men differed; that even after ratification it was not universally applauded, and that the Bill of Rights grew from specific demands made by some individuals and some conventions. One historian went so far, indeed, as to consider the Bill the fulfilling of pledges made by the Federalists during the campaign for ratification.

Understanding of the Constitution itself, it is hoped, will come from a double process: reading the document and the study of the document in the historical context from which it emerged.

Finally, the student should understand that different men have considered the Constitution in different ways and have reached different conclusions; that there are still major differences of opinion; that the framers have been pictured as everything from divinely inspired super-patriots to self-interested speculators suspicious of popular government and concerned primarily with securing their own investments. The student should not be allowed to make this divergence of opinion an escape from making his own assessment; rather these different views might be guides to arriving at a position, and they may be clues as to why the document has survived as long as it has. (i.e., Because it can be so many things to so many different people, the document itself has hardly ever been questioned. All that comes into question is its interpretation.)

The unit assumes that students know a little about the American Revolution and the events which led up to it. It also assumes a slight understanding of the political ideas which underlie the Declaration of Independence and which compose the English and American tradition of constitutional government. The Declaration of Independence appears as Appendix E in this booklet.

The unit begins with a generalized comment, proceeds through fragments of documentary evidence pertaining to various stages of the period, and concludes with a number of other generalizations. We follow a generally chronological structure, but we hope that the structure will prove logical as well as chronological.

The outline which follows can be applied to essays or class discussions or both. However, it is hoped that several short papers will be assigned. The discussions can be run in the form of debates or, preferably, as Socratic sessions with the teacher leading through his use of questions.

There is no need to have regular class sessions each day; part of the required meetings can be devoted to advance work on reading or writing assignments or to individual work with the students.

Monday: Section I assigned for reading in class. Questions for discussion, preferably in a 200 word composition:

What is your reaction to the quotation from the speech? Assuming you had read this statement in a history textbook, would you feel that it represented a worthwhile description of the subject with which it deals? If you feel you do not know enough to make a final judgment, what more would you like to know, and where might you go to find out? Turn in your paper at the end of class.

The idea here is merely to put the student on his own right away, to ask him to make a statement about the quotation and to begin working toward some notion of what history is and what the historian does. Our object is not to make historians; the object is merely to make the student think. Submitting papers at the end of class will give the teacher a chance to plan a discussion for the following day.

Section I can be used as a point of reference at any stage of the unit, but its main function is in helping to establish a definition of history (why the quotation is not good history) and in providing some idea about the use of sources, where they can be found, the likelihood of varied views in history, and the limits of any conclusion. There is no intention to be either "patriotic" or to have fun with the naïveté of the statement. The intent is merely to begin to differentiate between history and a comment on history.

The succeeding sections are planned for homework reading and discussion material, one section for each day, beginning with II for Tuesday. However, there is no absolute need to follow this day-by-day plan if other schedules seem more desirable.

Tuesday: Section II. From the Peace to the Convention (1783—87).

The object of this section is to present material similar to that used by historians to prove (a) that this was a "critical period" or (b) that it wasn't. It is also intended to show a little of the state of mind of those who eventually became the moving force behind the new Constitution. We wish to show here the sources of the Constitution and the sources of at least some of the opposition to it.

Questions:

Was this a "critical period"? What was the crisis about? What were the concerns of the nationalists of the period?

What kind of government did the Articles of Confederation provide? Where was control finally lodged, in the states or in the central government? Judging from the letters and documents, what were the failures and successes of the Confederation period? Do these documents present a conclusive picture or is there room for disagreement?

How does the material in Section II make you change your position from yesterday (assuming it did)? If it merely confirmed your position or if you feel the readings are not relevant, explain. What do you know now, that you did not know after reading Section I? What else would you want to know if you were writing your own history of the period about which you read?

In the course of this discussion, the teacher can point out that some historians, at least, listed a number of significant administrative achievements (i.e., the establishment of a bureaucracy or civil service); he might also suggest (especially if the traditional "critical period" argument seems to be accepted) that any war is likely to be followed by profound economic readjustments. The teacher, finally, might find it helpful to keep in mind some of the arguments made by the historians in Section VIII of the reading, merely for his own use in leading the discussions.

Wednesday and Thursday: Section III. The Constitution (1787). (The teacher may wish to take longer; he can do this by cutting one of the discussions.)

The intention of this section is not to teach Constitutional history or to demonstrate its implications for the question of the Bank of the United States or the Dred Scott decision. (The teacher may want to take more time and go into subsequent Constitutional history on his own.) The purpose of this material is to look at the Constitution as a product of its age and of the men who made it. To the extent that students understand the legal and governmental and philosophical sources, so much the better. Yet this is not the prime object here. The prime object is to make the student aware of the fact that the Constitution was a means to an end and that that end was a "more perfect union." It should be plain that such a union was by no means a certain thing in 1787. It should be pointed out that the succeeding sections all help clarify the text of the Constitution. Thus the teacher need not feel he must cover the whole subject at this particular time.

In going through the Constitution itself the most relevant sections for emphasis are probably:

The Preamble

Article I

    Section 2, Par. 3

    Section 3, Par. 1

    Section 8

    Section 9

    Section 10

Article II

    Section 1, Par. 1

    Section 2

Article III

    Section 1

    Section 2, Par. 1

Article IV

    Section 1

    Section 2

Article VI

In addition to discussing these articles individually, and with general reference to Section II in the manual, "The Critical Period," the teacher may wish to refer particularly to Madison's "vices" (Selection V). Thus Madison's first "vice" bears reference on Art. I, Sec. 8 (indeed many of Madison's complaints are in part answered here). Madison's eighth "vice" relates to the first part of Article VII (though the objection is not entirely met). Madison's second "vice" relates to Art. I, Sec. 10, etc.

The teacher, before going ahead, should review the material of the sections which follow since they, and especially Section IV (The Federalists), are highly relevant for the study of the Constitution itself. Indeed, one of the exciting things for the student may be the discovery of the consistencies between the nationalist complaints of 1783–87, the Constitution, and the Federalists' arguments for its adoption. He may thus discover for himself a pattern, a historical construct that he has made on his own.

It might be feasible to divide the discussion into two phases.

A) The Constitution as a response to the demands of the nationalists in the critical period.

Questions:

What were the prime objectives in drawing a new Constitution? How did the Constitution fulfill these objectives? From the material you have read to date, what would you conclude were the most important reasons for writing a new Constitution? What was its object? That is, how does the Constitution meet the demands made by Hamilton, Washington, Madison, and the other nationalists (or Federalists) that you have read? Be specific. What is the most important difference, as you see it, between the Constitution and the Articles of Confederation? How does it "improve" on the Articles of Confederation? If you feel it does not meet these demands, explain. Be sure to point out the limits of your conclusion by telling where you feel you do not have enough material to make a proper judgment. (For instance, you have not read all the documents pertaining to the period and you do not, presumably, know much at this point about the way the Constitution worked out in practice.)

B) The language of the Constitution:

Questions:

Does the preamble, and especially "We the people," signify a major change from the Articles? (It must be pointed out here that the wording was accidental, that it was included in this way because the framers had no idea which states would ratify.) *Does the Constitution provide a "national" or a "federal" government?* (Madison in Federalist #39 argued that it was neither wholly one or the other.) *Was judicial review intended?* (Hamilton argued in one number that it was, in another that it was not.) *If there was a shift from state to national power, how was it achieved in the Constitution? Is the wording of the Constitution final and definite, or is it open to interpretation?*

Friday: Section IV. *The Federalist:* arguments for ratification (1787–88). There is no need for the student to comprehend every word of these arguments. He should, however, be able to understand the general points that were made. To simplify references in discussion the paragraphs of #23 have been lettered.

Questions:

Federalist 2: *What does the writer assume about the natural condition of America? What does he, by implication, seem to want to avoid? Does it, therefore, seem to be inevitable in 1787–88 that the United States would be one nation? Would you say that Jay was a nationalist or a man committed to a decentralized confederacy?*

Federalist 23:

A) *What does "energetic" mean?*

C, D) The states are here accused of certain shortcomings, as is the Confederation as a whole. *What are they? Does the material in Section II of this booklet bear these charges out?*

C) *What does the writer mean about "legislating upon the States"? Do you have any evidence that this was, in fact, the system under the Confederation? What does the writer mean when he says "we must extend the laws of the federal government to the individual citizens . . . ?"*

E) *What do the words "simple," "compound," "sole," and "confederate" mean? How does the Constitution provide for a compound, confederate government? What specific powers does the writer feel necessary for the federal government? In what way do these powers mitigate the vices listed by Madison? In looking over this whole* excerpt from Federalist #23, what words would you say most aptly describe its subject? What does it advocate?

Federalist 51:

What is the writer talking about? What kind of charge is he trying to answer?

As you consider all three papers together, what would you say is the central argument of the Federalist series? As you read them, what would you expect to be the main objections to the Constitution in 1787–88? Taking together everything you have read so far, including, of course, the Constitution, what do you feel is the central concern of Washington, Jay, Madison, and Hamilton? What were their fears? Given the evidence you have, do you feel their fears were justified? Reconsider the statement you made about Section I. Do you feel it needs further revision? If so, what?

In leading the discussion, the teacher may also wish to make reference to *Federalist 10*, contained in the Appendix. This paper, Madison's classic dealing with factions, reveals a tremendous amount about the framers' view that self-interest, including economic interests, plays a vital part in public affairs.

Monday: Section V. The anti-Federalists: arguments against ratification, and a rebuttal.

There are two or three considerations here. (a) The readings should impress upon the student that ratification was not automatic: that men of ability and good intention opposed the Constitution. (b) That the nation was not united in its concern about the disintegration of the union. Please note that the major anti-Federalist argument is by Richard Henry Lee who is also represented in the readings on "The Critical Period." It might be fruitful to have the students refer back to his pre-Convention remarks to see how, in this case, a man's position seems to remain consistent through the period.

Questions for the Student:

Would you say that most of the men read in this section were concerned about the same things as Hamilton, Washington, or Madison? What were they concerned about? From what you remember about the Revolution and the events which preceded it, do you feel that the concerns expressed here are novel in American history? What is a "bill of rights"? Do you know where the idea of such a bill comes from? Considering the documents you have read, why wasn't such a bill of rights included? Do you feel that Hamilton's argument is satisfactory? If the failure to include a bill was an oversight, how do you account for it? If you feel there was no bill as a result of a deliberate decision, how do you account for that?

The discussion here, if successful, can be taken one step further, for after establishing the points at issue between Federalists and anti-Federalists, it would also be interesting to explore the points of agreement between them. It might also be possible to establish some notion of the view that the men of the age held about human nature; their suspicion of government and their rather low view of human nature. This is also a good point to revert to the quotation in Section I. That is, to show that the men of the age were practical, tough-minded, realistic, rather than idealistic.

Tuesday: Section VI. Pressure for a bill of rights and other amendments.

Questions:

Did ratification by nine states resolve the issues raised in the preceding months? On what criticisms of the Constitution did the anti-Federalists seem most united?

This discussion and Wednesday's can, to some extent, be telescoped if the discussions on the preceding days run over. The reading here is fairly light.

Wednesday: Section VII. The Bill of Rights.

Questions:

Look over the Bill of Rights, then go back over Sections V and VI. What fears of Patrick Henry, for example, would you expect the amendments to meet? Can you recall specific events in prior American history that help to explain the existence of Article I, Article II, etc.? How then, was the Bill of Rights a logical consequence of the events which preceded it? Did it satisfy all the demands for amendment? What demands were not met? Did all these demands concern individual rights or were other "rights" also at stake? How does the tenth amendment have a place in a "bill of rights"? Insofar as the Constitution and the Bill establish an American system of government how does that system determine the relation of citizen, state, and national government?

Thursday: Section VIII. Commentary.

Here are a number of comments about the Constitution, most of them by modern historians. Clearly students have not read enough to make any full evaluation of any of them. They merely appear to give the students some notion of the variety of interpretations that are possible. The quotations can be used in a great many ways: as guides to the student's own interpretation of the problem; as subjects for debate, as starting points for review essays of the whole problem.

The whole intent of the unit has been to work from the specific to the general, to set out landmarks at specific points and then connect them for a survey of the terrain.

Questions:

What were the attitudes about America and about the nature of politics in the 1780's and 1790's? What considerations prompted the new Constitution? What considerations prompted opposition to the

Constitution? On what did the Federalists and anti-Federalists agree; on what did they disagree? What generated demands for a Bill of Rights? Was the Bill of Rights a reaction to the Constitution, or was it generated by the same philosophy and attitudes that produced the Constitution itself?

The readings in Section VIII raise many direct questions for the student:

Which single author most nearly expresses your own point of view about the Constitution and its adoption? Tell why. If you disagree with him in any way or if you wish to add any comments of your own, go ahead and state your position. From this you can proceed to elaborate your own historical interpretation of the period. Defend it wherever possible with direct references to the material you have read in the past two weeks or to anything else that you know about American history.

What does one do in DOING history? What kind of evidence is most useful? What are the limitations of historical conclusions? Why does one make conclusions at all? Questions for the student are limitless. He might be set not only to making a kind of final generalization, but he might also compare it with his views at the beginning of the unit, then retrace the steps that brought him to his final point.

Friday: Section IX. The final day can be used to extend the discussion from the previous day, or it can be used for an examination, or both.

It is hard to estimate the speed at which the class will proceed during the course of the unit; perhaps it would even be possible to divide the class, to have some members working ahead of others. Discussions might be held on alternate days for the slow and fast learners. While one part of the class is engaged in discussion, perhaps another part can work on reading or writing.